Spotlight

on
Assessment in
Music Education

Spotlight
on
Assessment in
Music Education

MENC The National Association for Music Education

*MENC would like to thank the MEA state editors throughout the country,
who facilitate the distribution
of essential information to MENC members in their states.*

Copyright © 2001 by MENC: The National Association for Music Education
1806 Robert Fulton Drive
Reston, VA 20191-4348
All rights reserved.
Printed in the United States of America
ISBN 1-56545-143-0

Contents

The Spotlight series comprises articles that have appeared in magazines of MENC state affiliates over the past several years. The purpose of the series is to broaden the audience for the valuable work that is being done by music educators across the country. Were it not for the dedication of the state editors and article authors, this series would not be possible. MENC would like to thank these individuals for their contributions and to encourage others to share their expertise through MEA and MENC publications.

Introduction

Today, issues relating to accurate, authentic, and efficient assessment are being discussed by music educators all across the nation. Since the 1994 publication of the *National Standards for Arts Education* and the implementation of state standards that are based upon them, music programs are experiencing new demands for accountability. Now that the standards have clarified what students should know and be able to do, music educators are responding with the development of new methodologies for student assessment that are more fair, concrete, and goal-oriented.

Not that assessment is a new phenomenon in music education! Always a vital part of the teaching of music and performance skills, assessment has always meant more than having a grade to place on a student's report card. Proper evaluation provides students with useful feedback that facilitates better learning. Accurate assessment also helps teachers themselves to determine their level of success in instruction, giving direction to future trends in teaching methods.

Assessment with regard to the teaching of music has always had its particular difficulties and frustrations. Time limitations play an important role in these problems. Music teachers generally have a limited amount of time that they are able to spend with a multitude of students.

With rehearsals and performances beyond the confines of the regular school day, often for multiple ensembles, teachers also have difficulty finding the time in their busy schedules to grade papers or assess recordings. On top of this, assessment in music education is more complex than many other subjects because of the subjective nature of the criteria required for judging performance skills.

The authors of articles for *Spotlight on Assessment in Music Education* address these and other assessment issues relating to the value of assessments, the benefits and drawbacks of various forms of evaluation, and the essential components required for successful assessment techniques. Several authors offer their own specific strategies and rubrics, which can be modified to meet the needs of a variety of music education settings.

More than anything, this book is a compendium of the insights and experience of dedicated music educators who are sharing their perspectives with colleagues across the country. This professional interaction will inspire further exchange among music educators, in such venues as MENC journals, division and national conferences, and network communities, thereby lifting the profession together to higher goals and accomplishments.

Assessing Student Sight-Singing

by Stephan P. Barnicle

Now that the National Standards have been developed and discussed in every possible forum, the discussion has turned to "assessment." It seems that every professional gathering this year will be hosting sessions in an attempt to determine how we can go about assessing whether or not students are meeting any of these benchmarks set by the Standards.

In formal and informal gatherings I have heard several of our colleagues ask how we might best assess the progress of our own students in our performing ensembles in this area. This is a question I have long been dealing with as well, and I offer a couple of suggestions I have found to be successful.

Again, in discussing "music technology," all of the answers need not come from the latest developments or the costliest of equipment. In fact, often the best solution is the simplest and least expensive. For example, how to best test students' sight-singing ability? The simplest answer is probably to hand students a piece of music you are certain is unfamiliar to them and ask them to sing it for you.

Assessment, however, implies that you will be able to collect this data for evaluation and comparison to other data at a later time. The "data" in this case would be the student's initial performance of the music. The best way I have found to "collect" such data is to record the performance.

A "data gathering" situation may look like this. Set up a tape recorder with a microphone in a room adjacent to your rehearsal room or classroom. Provide a table and two chairs: one chair for the student being "tested," the other for the "monitor" who will operate the recorder and read the procedural instructions to the student. (The monitor might be an "aide," a "practice teacher," or a student who has already completed the exercise.) On the table, provide the music to be "sight-sung." In order to assure unfamiliarity, compose the exercise yourself. This assures that you are testing the ability to sight-sing at the level of difficulty you intend (see figure 1. Sight-Singing Sample Exercise).

Instructions can be given to all students before the process begins, as well as by the monitor to each individual student. The students may leave your rehearsal room or classroom one at a time, entering the test room. When they sit at the table they are given the allotted time (either unlimited, or a specific time frame, depending on your "task construction guidelines") to look over the music before performing. When they are ready to perform their "answer" they indicate to the monitor

Figure 1. Sight-Singing Sample Exercise

who will start the tape. When they finish, they leave and another student enters and follows the same procedure. When all students have performed, you will have the performances captured on tape for later evaluation.

Some suggestions:

- Have the monitor assign a number to each student as they enter and ask the student to announce their number after starting recording and before performing their "answer." This will allow you later to score each answer without prejudice. The monitor records the number by the student's name for later reference.
- To truly consider it "sight-singing" a good rule-of-thumb is to give each student as much time to study the material beforehand as it should take to perform the piece in real time at performance tempo.
- The first time this is done you might consider giving unlimited (within reason) preparation time to help you get a benchmark for the actual ability of the students to accomplish such a task.
- If you prefer, the exercise may be accompanied by prerecording an accompaniment tape and recording the answer through a mixer either together with the accompaniment track(s) or on a separate track.

Evaluation can include assessment of group skills and/or individual skill level. It can be as simple as "Yes" (they performed correctly), "Close" (they demonstrated an educated guess, but were not totally accurate), or "No" (they had no idea what they were doing) scored for both rhythmic and pitch accuracy. Or you may wish to design a rating scale with any number of criteria, which can be evaluated as specifically as you wish (and your time allows).

Long-term, portfolio-type assessment becomes possible. You might prepare an individual cassette tape of each student beginning in elementary school which will contain such data all the way through high school, recording not only growth in sight-singing, but also vocal development and other vocal/choral skills.

More recent technology can assist you in refining the evaluation of this data. Now that sequencers commonly include digital audio capabilities, it is fairly simple to sequence parts or accompaniment to a song and ask students to sight-sing into the microphone, making a digital recording. This can be translated into notation that will show exactly how closely a student comes to the correct reading.

Some recent software will allow you to tutor students in sight-singing and also provide tests to measure the accuracy of response both rhythmically and tonally. These programs will usually provide for testing and automatic record-keeping right on the computer.

Stephan P. Barnicle teaches music at Simsbury High School in Simsbury, Connecticut. This article, which appears here in condensed and updated form, originally appeared in the Winter 1996 issue of Connecticut's CMEA News. Reprinted by permission.

What Does a Grade of S, N, or U Mean to Parents?

by Karen Bouton

In many school districts across Florida, elementary music teachers are limited in the grades they can assign for student progress. One reason given for the use of the grades Satisfactory, Needing Improvement or Unsatisfactory reflects the short amount of time students actually spend in the discipline of music. How can we, as teachers of a very important part of the curriculum, extend or expand these grades so that parents understand what we teach and how their children honestly perform on tasks involving musical skill?

One possible solution is a simple version of authentic assessment. By analyzing the content of our classes and consistently observing our students, we can quickly and easily present students and parents with an accurate assessment of their progress. By using such an instrument for assessments, students and parents can have a better understanding of our expectations. They will also have information that will help them progress and improve as they further their music education.

An authentic assessment instrument can be as simple or complex as you desire and can be expanded and changed over the time. You might begin by simply including singing skills, playing instruments, reading music, creating/writing music, and movement activities. A separate area can include behavior, participation in class, and absences. This documentation can be made easy by using a separate file folder for each class and stapling an updated roster into it at the beginning of each grading period (see figure 1).

During each class, simply walk around and quickly evaluate each child by observation. Code these observations on the roster using something simple. An "M" or "+" could be used for a skill that has been mastered. John Feierabend's term "emerging" ("E") is a wonderful way to describe skills that we are confident a child will secure in the near future. "H" could be used to indicate that the child needs extra help in a specific area. Staying away from traditional grading scales for music skills protects students from feeling inferior if they don't get straight "A's." Whatever "Codes" or "Grades" you use is your choice, but make sure the codes are explained on the assessment that goes home to parents (see figure 2). Evaluations of participation, behavior, and care of equipment can be in terms of a traditional S, N, or U, since expectations for these behaviors are the same in any subject area of the elementary curriculum.

Obviously, there are some excellent reasons for authentic assessment in music. Parents can determine how their children are improving throughout the year and can learn very early if their child is having a problem in a certain area. This will also help classroom teachers, because true learning difficulties are usually reflected across the curriculum. Our consistent documentation can be used to identify children who need additional help, and many parents will realize very quickly if intervention is needed at home. Parents and students alike will also come to the conclusion that attendance and participation in music class are important if we, as teachers, are willing to keep up with the absences and progress of literally hundreds of students.

Karen W. Bouton teaches music at Graceville Elementary School (a Florida Department of Education "2001 Music Demonstration School") in Graceville, Florida. This article originally appeared in the April 1998 issue of Florida Music Director. *Reprinted by permission.*

Figure 1. Example of Authentic Assessment Instrument

		Absences									Singing		Playing		Reading		Movement		Creating		Discipline	
#	Name	1	2	3	4	5	6	7	8	9	S	S	P	P	R	R	M	M	C	C	D	D
1																						
2																						
3																						
4																						
5																						
6																						
7																						
8																						
9																						
10																						
11																						
12																						
13																						
14																						
15																						
16																						
17																						
18																						
19																						
20																						
21																						
22																						
23																						
24																						
25																						
26																						
27																						
28																						
29																						
30																						

Figure 2. Example of Assessment Form to Parents

Student Name _____   Homeroom Teacher _____

Singing Skills   M = Student has mastered presented material.

_____ Playing Instruments   E = Student has emerging skills.

_____ Movement   H = Student shows difficulty in mastering this

_____ Reading Music   skill. Additional help is needed.

_____ Creating Music   S = Student is very disciplined in this area.

_____ Participates totally in class   N = Student needs improvement.

_____ Obeys class rules   U = Student is unsatisfactory in this area.

_____ Takes care of equipment

_____ Absences/Tardiness*

(out of 9 weeks)

_____ Conference required

*Absences and tardiness are often a result of incomplete homework or class work. Music classes meet only once each week, so attendance is very important if progress is to be made. If excessive absences are indicated, please encourage the student and check to make sure work is completed on time.

Assessment: Pencil, Paper ... & Performance, Too!

by Ann A. Burbridge

Assessment is like taking a snapshot of student performance at determined points of instruction. Just like real photographs, these snapshots can be taken in bright or dim light, with a fixed-angle or wide-angle lens, and with the focus sharp or blurred. How the picture is taken affects the resulting quality of the image we see. The picture of student performance we capture is a direct result of our choices in assessment tools. Pencil-and-paper tests give us an idea of how students are doing, but the result may be a snapshot with limited view, dim and fuzzy. On the other hand, performance-based, or "rubric," tests provide a far more accurate view. They open up the wide-angle lens to focus on the whole student and give us, as teachers, a clear, bright assessment of that student's abilities. The kind of assessment we use depends on what picture we want to see. What should the end result of music study be, and how will assessment help us make it better? Will a pencil-and-paper test measure musicianship, skill attainment or artistic control in making music? These types of considerations and questions will help us evaluate our programs and instructional methods.

Music teachers often see 300 to 800 students in three to seven grades. This setup requires them to teach up to seven age-appropriate and sequenced curricula. This alone can scare many music teachers away from testing and assessing their students in a formal fashion. It appears that teachers have avoided testing in the affective domain. The emergence of aesthetic studies in music allowed us to state that we can't test feelings and matters of personal taste. When we did test, it was usually a pencil-and-paper test that only assessed a student's knowledge of theory and music history, that is, how many beats are in a half note and name five characteristics of music from the Baroque era. These test items are important to the development of music knowledge, but they do not measure the essence of music: music-making, musicianship and artistry.

When we are only tested on sentence structure or the definition of nouns and verbs in English class, we are not encouraged to master what all of these grammar skills could produce: writing and high levels of understanding in literature. Likewise, in music class, if we place the emphasis only on the mechanics of music, the importance of musicality is forsaken. Did Mozart have to master the skills of recognizing note values and singing in solfège in order to begin the process of composing music? Knowing note values and singing solfège are important tools in music class, but they are not the end product of musicianship. Up until now we have been at a primitive level of music assessment in many music classes, testing a skill or drill out of the context of music-making. Assessment for most music teachers can be haphazard, at best.

We can continue going down the path of nonassessment or haphazard and inaccurate testing, or we can begin using an assessment tool that will test learning in the context of music-making and musicianship. If we don't assess, then our students are aimlessly rambling in our music classes. If we do assess, then we must find the best practices in music education and start applying them to raise the level of music teaching in Texas. The best assessment tool to accomplish this goal is the rubric. Rubric assessment brightens the snapshot by shedding light on the student's music-making ability. The ASCD (The Best of Educational Leadership, 1997) defines a rubric as a scoring tool that lists the criteria for a piece of work or "what counts" (for example, purpose, organization, details, voice, and mechanics are often what count in a piece of writing); it also articulates gradations of quality for each criterion, from excellent to poor. A variety of performance skills and techniques can be assessed with a rubric, instead of just one or two. This testing tool aims a wide-angle lens at everything involved in music-making, not just a handful of areas. Once we have a well-lit, complete view of a student's musicianship, the rubric puts the picture into sharp focus. Assessing students based on performance is not just for secondary music, it is necessary and applicable for all age levels, beginning in kindergarten.

The new TEKS are performance-based, requiring children to make music and not just to learn about music. This emphasis on performance requires having skills and techniques ready in the classroom to make the best music at each age level. In my classroom I have experimented with rubric assessment. Before I moved to this kind of performance-based assessment, I grappled with the end results of a classroom focused only on narrow,

"testable" concepts. My students knew these concepts and could master tests of note values, hand signs and mallet technique, but something was missing; the tests did not elicit musicianship from my students. Therefore, I changed the focus of my elementary classes by making my assessment performance-based. The note values, hand signs and mallet techniques took on new importance as my students learned to make music instead of memorizing concepts. Rubric assessment encourages this behavior by testing the skills and artistry necessary for a musical rendering of a piece. Now, instead of a concept-driven classroom, I have students learning musically. When we begin assessing in a manner that produces artistic music making, we will highlight the value of music in Texas education.

TEKS: Rubric Example

Students in grades 2–6 prepare a song learning the text, rhythm, solfège and the appropriate conducting pattern. In cooperative learning groups that I call "ensembles," the students work on musicianship to perform the memorized song at the end of the six weeks. The students learn and rehearse the quality features throughout the six weeks, and then are given a checklist (see figure 1) to assess their success before the rubric is used. The checklist is an excellent way for students to grasp the big picture of what the finished product should sound like. The rubric (see figure 2) is used at the

---

Figure 1. Checklist I*

Student _____ Date _____

Title/Topic <u>Singing Assessment Preparation</u> **Class** _____ **Teacher** <u>Mrs. Burbridge</u> _____

Prompt: Sings assigned memory song with clear and light singing; in tune and on pitch; enunciates vowels and consonants, expressively; exhibits teamwork in ensemble

Standard: TEKS: Creative Expression/Performance: The student sings individually and in groups, performing a varied repertoire of music.

Quality Features	Student	Peer	Teacher
Singing Register			
Clear and Light Quality			
Memorized			
Stays on Pitch			
Correct Intervals			
Enunciated Vowels and Consonants			
Musicianship/Expressive			
Teamwork			
On Task			
Productive and Efficient			

Targeted Results: Artistic performance

*Strategic Learning Strategies, Inc., 1996–98.

end of the grading period, demonstrating musical skills and higher-level thinking skills to produce a musical "product." Each ensemble is given a chance to warm up before performing for the class. I involve the students in the discussion of each area of assessment to give the students ownership of their progress. I use other checklists and rubrics for other areas of the TEKS. These tools are a work-in-progress as I learn to apply the TEKS and assess student progress authentically in a performance context vs. pencil-and-paper tests.

It is time to put our scrapbook of fuzzy photos on the shelf. Our new picture album is ready to be filled with the brightest, best-focused, wide-angle snapshots of student musicianship. Performance-based assessment is the latest issue in music education that has us looking at the big picture in Texas and providing our students with the best possible learning environment. Openness to research and learning about new ways to assess our students will strengthen our position as educators.

Ann A. Burbridge is choir director at Madison High School in the North East Independent School District in San Antonio, Texas. This article originally appeared in the Fall 1998 issue of Texas' TMEC Connections. Reprinted by permission.

Figure 2. Scoring Rubrics—Level 5*

Student _____ **Date** _____

Title/Topic <u>Singing Rubric</u>   **Class** _____ **Teacher** <u>Mrs. Burbridge</u>

Prompt: Sings assigned memory song with clear and light singing; in tune and on pitch; enunciates vowels and consonants, expressively; exhibits teamwork in ensemble

Standard: TEKS: Creative Expression/Performance: The student sings individually and in groups, performing a varied repertoire of music.

Performance	All of the Time	Most of the Time	Some of the Time	Not Yet	Does Not Try
Singing Register: Uses Singing Voice					
Pitched Singing: Stays on Pitch					
Vocal Quality: Clear and Light Singing					
Text: Memorized with Enunciated Vowels and Consonants					
Musicianship: Expressive Singing					
Teamwork					

Targeted Results: Students will give an artistic performance of memory song.

*Strategic Learning Strategies, Inc., 1996–98

Musicianship Tests Improve Performance and Grade Credibility

by John Carmichael

The high goal of high-level performance motivates many band directors in rehearsal. What actually is high-level performance could certainly be debated, but how to achieve it is a matter for careful consideration. Everything starts with a sound philosophy of music education as expressed through the band medium. My personal goals have been to teach a thoughtful love for music and to provide the literacy skills with which the student may access music independently. The process of achieving those goals has always been more important than the final product.

In previous articles, I have addressed the best way to measure one's success in achieving the aforementioned goals and how to make a strong connection with the art of music, thus increasing the chance of producing feelingful responses in the student. One concern mentioned is the issue of correctness in performance and how to obtain it.

In the typical rehearsal setting, it is possible to produce a reasonable facsimile of a composer's intent without effectively addressing the fundamental problems of individual players. It is nothing more than an approximation. This holistic approach, when used with the average band, sacrifices the full aesthetic potential of a fully accurate performance, complete with consistent pitch center, resonant harmonies, rhythmic tightness and, most of all, musical sensitivity. In a way, it represents the "dumbing down" so often referred to in education and related areas.

It also does not allow for a music teacher to account for the individual student's musical progress as he or she participates in a band program over time. Musicianship tests provide a framework with which one may not only improve the fundamental skills of every player, but also track every student's musical development. Furthermore, musicianship tests represent the very best way I know to hold students individually accountable for practice and preparation.[1]

The concept did not originate with me. The first employment of such a system, to my knowledge, occurred at Winter Park High School in Winter Park, Florida.[2] Jack Williams was the conductor, and he was well-known for running an instrumental music program that was not only literacy-based, but also highly successful in performance. My first encounter with a musicianship-test program in practice was during my student teaching and first year of employment at Leon High School in Tallahassee, Florida. That program was directed by F. Lewis Jones and was regarded as one of the most consistently superior bands in Florida. The forms provided with this article are directly based upon forms developed by Lewis Jones. I carried this system with me to Lakeland High School and attribute much of that band program's success to the individual attention students received while completing musicanship test requirements.

The following are considerations for musicianship test deployment:

1. The musicianship test must be graduated for each year in band. This addresses administrative concerns about the justification for taking essentially the same course for three or four

consecutive years. For the sake of this article, and by the way of past experience, I propose the following configuration: 4th class for freshmen, 3rd class for sophomores, 2nd class for juniors, 1st class for seniors, and Master for advanced placement/college prep. level.

2. Musicianship tests may be used as qualifiers for awards and membership in different bands (if you have more than one, of course). At Lakeland High School, a student must have completed the 2nd Class Musicianship Test to be eligible for membership in the Wind Ensemble.

3. Musicianship tests may be used as the basis for the grade assigned during any grading period. For example, to receive an "A" for the grading periods of the second semester, a student must complete the appropriate test by the end of the first semester.

4. The only effective way to motivate students to prepare individually is to make them individually accountable. Musicianship tests do this better than any other method.

5. Musicianship tests may be tailored to the director's expectations (which may be either too high or too low). Most beneficially, the tests can be redefined after a year or so to allow for increased expectations and general program improvement.

6. A beauty of this system is that a test may not be failed—it can only be passed or not passed. Since a student may come in as many times as it takes to complete a test (something a director might want to refine due to time constraints), they are virtually guaranteed some level of success.

7. A file folder could be made for each student in which all records pertaining to that person might be kept. This would make retrieval of data regarding academic (as well as behavioral and administrative) information easy. For those who are not computer-challenged, an electronic filing system could be developed.

8. This system makes participation in band eminently more defensible from the academic side, and thereby helps to ensure band's place in the curriculum. It also makes a band grade usable for computation of grade point average.[3]

The Downside

It takes a lot of time—a whole lot of time. There are several ways that one might be able to lessen the load without decreasing system effectiveness.

1. Let those who have completed the first-class test be qualified to pass off some of the requirements on lower level tests. This fosters ownership of the program and a kind of prestige for those who achieve the status of "teacher."

2. Private teachers may be used to help pass off requirements. In time, if you are observant and a good musician, you will be able to discern which teachers to trust and which not to trust.

3. Decrease the number of after-school rehearsals. The benefit you will achieve by working with students individually will more than make up for missed rehearsal time. The student will actually spend less time in band (and thus have less to complain about),[4] and more time preparing individually. The director, initially, will spend more time at the bandroom, but this should decrease somewhat as the system becomes fully integrated into the program. Beside the very positive gain of better performance skills by the students, there will also be the wonderful benefit of getting to know the band members as individuals. As the students become more competent and independent, they will begin to enjoy the experience of playing music on their instruments.

Other Considerations

1. The private time scheduled with students should not be their practice time. Your role as teacher could degenerate into that of a personal trainer if allowed to do so. Rather, strive to provide students with the skills to prepare the material themselves. Show them how to do it, but expect them to prepare the assignment to an acceptable level on their own.

2. Since you will be increasing the one-on-one time with students, it would be judicious to consider legal concerns. In short, you should be sure that the situation in which you administer the test will leave you above reproach.[5]

3. The success of the musicianship test in terms of improving performance levels will be a direct reflection of your musical values and standards. By using the system, you at least facilitate the opportunity to impart those values on an individual basis.

Figure 1 is an example of the 2nd class musicianship test. This is the level that I usually administered to juniors.

Once implemented, the musicianship test system will produce rapid gains in performance ability for your program. Although it is initially time-intensive, the musical rewards received will provide more than enough incentive to make such a

Figure 1. Lakeland High School Band 2nd Class Musicianship Test

Student _____ Instrument _____ Grad _____ Year _____

Date Completed _____ By _____

Requirements

_____ 1. Play from memory all major scales and arpeggios in accordance with the All-State instructions, quarter note = 120, two octaves where possible.

_____ 2. Be able to count all rhythms on the 2nd Class rhythm sheet.

_____ 3. Play a chromatic scale covering the practical range of your instrument in accordance with All-State requirements.

_____ 4. Play from memory the following harmonic minor scales and arpeggios for one octave in the same manner as the major scale: Concert C, G, D.

_____ 5. Demonstrate ability to prepare a selected musical exercise with attention to all musical detail.

_____ 6. Write a 300-word paper on the history and development of your instrument.

_____ 7. Perform accurately a sight-reading selection to the director's satisfaction.[a]

_____ 8. Pass with a minimum score of 80% on the written test given at the end of the semester.

Percussion Requirements

Omit #5 and #6 from above.

_____ 1. Perform accurately selected exercises from the Podemski Snare Drum Method.

_____ 2. Play any snare drum solo, grade III or higher, to the director's satisfaction.

_____ 3. Perform accurately a selected mallet instrument exercise to the director's satisfaction.

_____ 4. Perform accurately a selected timpani exercise to the director's satisfaction.

_____ 5. Complete the last 14 rudiments, open-close-open, as adopted by the N.A.R.D.

[a]The Watkins-Farnum Performance Scale, Forms A and B, is a standardized sight-reading achievement test that works quite nicely for this purpose. It is published by Hal Leonard.

Note. Copies of all test levels and the corresponding rhythm sheets may be found at the following web site: www.wku.edu/Dept/Academic/AHSS/Music/Mtests.html

---

test program an integral, ongoing part of a successful instrumental music program.

Notes

1. Public practice hour charts and signed forms from a parent to account for practice only provide opportunities for dishonesty. The only other choice is for students to play in front of their peers during class—something that tends to associate membership in band with humiliation and fear (not a particularly good thing).

2. Undoubtedly, there have been other similar systems in use. This statement only reflects my experience.

3. In many school systems, grades from music performance classes are thrown out of grade point average computations because the grades are based on participation only.

4. The main thing students complain about regarding rehearsal is wasted time. That is the time they sit in band doing nothing while waiting for the director to prepare the parts for other students. Music is its own best reward, and making music competently is positively addictive.

5. For example, leave the windows of your office uncovered so not only will people be able to see in while you administer the test, you will be able to keep an eye on your facility.

John Carmichael is associate professor of music education and director of bands at Western Kentucky University in Bowling Green. This article originally appeared in the May 2000 issue of Kentucky's Bluegrass Music News. *Reprinted by permission.*

Music Teaching and Assessment

by Richard K. Fiese and Robin E. Fiese

Education at large, and music education in particular, face a continuing assault on purpose, procedures, and products. We, as individuals and collectively as a profession, are feeling the attack on a very personal level. Students, parents, building-level and district administrators, even some within music education, assail us from differing directions and perspectives.

One of the areas that has been of great interest and attention on the part of those on the offensive, especially those who wear the mantle of education "reformers," has been the area of assessment. Much of this concern has been due, in part, to the fact that with all of the attention that has been focused on the development and adoption of educational standards, the profession is now duty-bound to develop a method of determining whether and to what extent students are achieving with respect to the established standards. Furthermore, education has in the meantime been insidiously forced into an industrial model, whereby efficiency is substituted for both quality and effectiveness and where the financial "bottom-line" seems to rule decisions that are more appropriately made for pedagogical reasons. This mindset ignores that institutions of education were never intended to be "successful businesses" in and of themselves, but rather environments where others, namely students and teachers, can be successful. Nevertheless, this represents much of current thinking in education.

We are in the "business" of enhancing the musical skills and knowledge of the students in our charge. That is the purpose of music teaching. Whether and to what extent our students are meeting this purpose is the "business" of assessment. It is not something that is done in addition to teaching; it is an integral part of "teaching." In fact, in the absence of assessment, we are unable to determine if our students are actually improving their musical skills and knowledge about music. However, it is important to remember that assessment is not a goal; it is simply a tool. It is the tool by which we make determinations regarding the musical behaviors of our students. In a very broad sense, the job of a music teacher is to monitor and elicit change regarding the musical behaviors of our students. Since the decisions that we make regarding our students are important (sometimes life-altering), we need to have information that is accurate, relevant, and relatively comprehensive. **If you believe that what you teach is important and how you teach is important, then what and how you assess what you teach is no less important because it is all one process.**

Surely teachers have always had a good idea of how well a class is progressing, who is doing well, who is in need of additional support, who works well in a group, who is keeping up and who is not. These observations are made on a daily basis perhaps a thousand times a day or more. These informal, implicit observations are important for teachers because it is part of the process of instructional flow. However, this information can be largely subjective (i.e., it is more likely to change from observer to observer) and since it is informal there is no reliable way to communicate these observations to the students, the parents, the administration, or to other decision-makers in the community. **This is one of the primary goals of assessment: To generate and communicate useful information for educational decision-making.** Therefore, teachers do not really need to do anything remarkably or substantially different regarding the process they already do when informally assessing students. Rather, teachers merely need to *make formal* and *explicit,* that which they already make *informal* and *implicit.* Such formal and explicit information can enhance *communication* regarding the music education of any teacher's students. To accomplish this communication implicates some systematic process so that information can be collected consistently and regularly for it to be reported consistently and regularly. This permits comparisons to be made between and among individuals, different classes, and the students' performance during successive years. Such comparisons of student information help teachers and other curriculum planners to improve the instructional delivery system, thereby hopefully improving student performance.

It is easy for us to become transfixed on the *process of teaching,* while ignoring the *products of learning.* We become concerned with the details of the instructional process without exercising the same care in determining if the students have actually learned the content. Assessment can become an afterthought ("If I have time left over during rehearsal") or something educationally extraneous done because of administrative demands ("We have to have six grades for every six weeks").

Assessment should enhance instruction, not interfere with it. While not every single aspect of instruction needs to be assessed, music teachers need to be vigilant in making certain that they are planning to assess those behaviors that define the essence of the instructional goals. As such, assessment should not focus on minutia, but rather on important instructional outcomes. It is easier to develop a musical "terms" test in a pencil-and-paper format than it is to deal with assessing more creative, productive, and musically substantive behaviors such as *performance* or *improvisation.* However, following the easy path does not lead to the most meaningful information.

It should also be recognized that all important educational outcomes cannot be assessed in the same manner or using the same, or similar, tools. Fitting the assessment task to the instructional outcome is crucial. Moreover, the more options a teacher has for assessment, the greater the options exist for instruction. The adage that "if all you have is a hammer, pretty soon everything begins to look like a nail" fits well for assessment as well.

Recently, there has been much debate about so-called "traditional" (here most equate *traditional* with pencil-and-paper tests) and alternative or "authentic" assessment. While such discussions are

fodder for graduate students and college professors seeking to occupy their time, the demarcations are not as clear as the purported "battle-lines" might suggest. The term "authentic" when used in conjunction with assessment is neither new nor all that "alternate." I submit that if an assessment is inauthentic, it is also most likely invalid. That is, it is unlikely that if the assessment task does not conform to the instructional goal (in format, substance, and presentation), then the assessment task is not really assessing the targeted behavior. Good pencil-and-paper tests exist and can be developed that assess specific kinds of skills and knowledge. Just because it is traditional does not make it invalid or useless. We in education are too quick to reject a tool because some new tool has been developed. Novelty should never be substituted for effectiveness.

So, for both traditional and authentic assessment the basic idea is that an assessment's tasks should be congruent with the manner of instruction and the nature of the subject matter. In music, students should be asked to create, produce, or perform something related to what is done in class. In doing so they are assumed to be involved with complex problem solving, and the tasks summon forth realistic (so-called "real-world") applications. Such *activities* are commonplace in the music classroom and rehearsal hall. In fact, it can be argued that the only areas of instruction in the typical curriculum where one encounters the "real world" are music and physical education. Many in the profession have been quick to announce that music education is "ahead" of the other academic areas with respect to authentic assessment and that authentic assessment is the harbinger of validating all that music educators do and have done in the classroom. This is a gross misstatement. We have been involved in authentic instructional activities from time immemorial, but that does not mean that we have reliably established criteria by which student performances are to be judged. Those who cite "contest" and "festival" ratings as evidence of music education's leadership in the area of authentic assessment overlook the notorious lack of reliable criteria (not to mention the reliability of judging the criteria and the challenges to validity regarding the "contest" and the instruction in the classroom). The development of appropriate and reliable criteria is the "sticky wicket" of authentic assessment for music education. It is problematic, but the difficulties do not excuse us from confronting and developing solutions to the problems.

It is important to remember that most of music instruction is based on developing the skills necessary for informed musical independence by our students. As such, the demands of the musical score provide the important educational outcomes and the essence of our appropriate assessment tasks (whether the "score" is "Hot Cross Buns" or the Hindemith Symphony). When developing an assessment, rely on the important musical outcomes found in the context of the music itself and you are likely to be "right on target."

Irrespective of the label that one places on his or her assessment, the following are good guideposts for the development of any assessment:

- Determine what types of skills and other knowledge students are to develop as a result of instruction. (The State and National Standards and district curriculum guides are good starting places. So are the music scores used for instruction.)
- Develop specific tasks whereby students can demonstrate these skills and this knowledge. (Use activities and tasks that relate to what students already do in class.)
- Develop clearly-stated criteria and standards for judging student performance.
- Develop a rating process that is "reliable" and relatively free from bias. (Given the same criteria and the same samples of behaviors, would Ms. Smith assess the students the same as did I?)
- Make certain that the purpose of the assessment is consistent with the use of the information gathered and that the information gathered is used in a manner consistent with the purpose.
- Take multiple samples of student "performance" over time. (More "snapshots" provide a better total picture.)
- Develop a reporting system so that the information gathered can be shared by those who need to know. (Develop a separate music "report card" in addition to the "one-letter" grade on the traditional report card.)

Any subject as vast and as complex as is assessment cannot be served by a single article, magazine issue, or even book. The discussions of the philosophical, technical, and practical aspects of assessment could easily fill hundreds of volumes.

Richard K. Fiese is professor of music education at Houston Baptist University in Houston, Texas; Robin E. Fiese is band director at Oak Ridge High School in Conroe, Texas. This article originally appeared in the September 1999 issue of Florida Music Director. *Reprinted by permission.*

Performance Assessment: Applications for General Music

by Briana Foley

The *National Standards for Arts Education*[1] was the impetus that changed the path of music education. Since then, states, including Florida, have developed models[2] which align curriculum and student expectations to achievement and content standards for music. The development of state standards, in turn, has motivated local districts to develop and implement expectations that emphasize high student achievement in music.[3] Music educators now face the challenge of designing sound assessments[4] that will meet the requirements set in these standards.

"If you always do what you always did, then you'll always get what you always got."[5] While music education is viewed as a performance-based discipline, music educators must reach beyond assessing only "performing" (singing and playing instruments) if music is to maintain its place as core in the curriculum. Whereas "performing" is an integral part of learning music, it is not the only means by which standards are assessed. Effective performance assessment methods target *skills,* as well as *factual and applicative knowledge, problem-solving and reasoning proficiency, the ability to create products,* and *dispositions.*[6]

This article is intended as an overview to the assessment process. Sound assessments, whether designed for music or other disciplines, share common attributes. The goal is to examine these characteristics and demonstrate their application for general music.

Defining Assessment

To determine what assessment is, it may be helpful to establish what it is not.

Assessment is not:
- a one-time event.
- a pass-fail grade.
- always pencil-and-paper.
- always teacher-directed.

Assessment is:
- a system which drives instruction forward.
- a continuous process which measures student academic growth.
- often multifaceted, involving more than one assessment method.
- often derived from student reflections.

The assessment process involves three components: test, measurement, and evaluation.[7] A *test* is a method used to examine what content a student has learned over a given period of time. Tests, in this context, may include both conventional (pencil-and-paper) and unconventional (performance, personal-communication) types. The information obtained from the test will be used to measure student academic growth and success. *Measurement* involves collecting, organizing, and analyzing test data. Measurement is dictated by specific criteria (rubrics, checklists) used to create the test. The third component, *evaluation,* implies placing value (a grade or rating) on a student's work based on the test measures.

Why Assess?

Perhaps the most important question before designing an assessment is to ask, "What purpose will this assessment serve?" There are two reasons teachers assess: (1) to diagnose and address the instructional needs of students and (2) to determine if a student has mastered content or is proficient in a standard. Regardless of the reason, the ultimate goal is to drive instruction forward. When assessment is used for diagnostic reasons, it is considered *formative*. Formative assessments are continuous and occur as part of everyday classroom instruction. *Summative* assessments, as suggested above, often measure a range of student learning and may be associated with a final grade. The assessment purpose directs assessment design. Sound assessments ensure that design supports the purpose.

Assessment Targets and Methods

Paralleled with the "why" of the assessment is the "what" and "how" of the assessment. The "what" refers to the achievement target[8] or focus. If the target is to assess *Read and notate music,*[9] for example, it must be clearly defined for the assessment to be effective. Listing the full range of benchmarks and competencies (skills, knowledge, and behaviors) eliminates ambiguity in the test and allows the student a better "shot" at the target.

The "how" concerns assessment method. The method must align with what is being assessed. In other words, choose the right tool for the job. Typical tests, even demanding ones, tend to over-assess student "knowledge" and under-assess student "know-how" with knowledge.[10] For example, *Selected Response* methods (multiple choice, true/false, short answer, and fill-in-the-blank) generally target recall of factual knowledge and, therefore, offer a limited view of a student's intellectual ability. When questions are constructed to include knowledge application, this method is more effective.

When a demonstration of knowledge use is required, *essay, personal communication,* or *performance* methods may be employed. *Essays* rely on written communication as the basis for assessing student achievement, while *personal communication* involves oral examinations, interviews, conferences, and conversations. *Performance* methods are used to measure skills, products and processes. For the target, *Read and notate music,* a demonstration of performance skills is required; the method which best aligns with the target is *performance*. It is important to note, however, that assessment can be multifaceted; more than one method may be applied.

Designing Sound Assessments

Assessment is not a one-time event, disjointed from instruction. Assessment works best when it

reveals strengths and weaknesses in student performance—when it suggests concrete action on the part of teacher and/or student.[11] Effective teachers involve students in the assessment process. When students have a clear understanding of what "success" means, they are able to take control of their learning and become better performers. Clarification of expectations is crucial to strong assessment design.

A sound design supports the purpose, reflects a clear target aligned with the best methods, offers a representative sample so that conclusions about student achievement are accurate, and accounts for bias and distortions.[12] Once these assumptions are in place, an assessment can be formulated.

Applications for General Music

The attributes of assessment design can be applied to any content area. The sidebar Assessment Blueprint demonstrates how they may apply to a general music assessment.

Future Thoughts

Creating sound assessments will be central to teaching music in the 21st century. As curriculum is shaped by achievement standards, the demand for tools to assess these standards will be greater than ever. Music educators must accept the challenge to teach and assess all aspects of standard-based curriculum. Only then will students be able to aim at clear targets, enabling them to hit the mark of the highest student achievement.

Notes

1. MENC. (1996). *Performance Standards for Music: Strategies and Benchmarks for Assessing Progress toward the National Standards, Grades PreK–12.* Reston, VA: Author.

2. Florida Department of Education. (1996). *The Arts: PreK–12 Sunshine State Standards and Instructional Practice.* Tallahassee, FL: Author.

3. Pinellas County Schools. (1996). *Pinellas County Schools Student Expectations for Music K–12.* Largo, FL: Author.

4. Stiggins, R. J. (1997). *Student-Centered Classroom Assessment,* 2nd edition. Upper Saddle River, NJ: Prentice Hall.

5. McClanahan, E., and Wicks, C. (1997). *Future Force: Kids That Want to, Can, and Do!* CA: Pact Publishing.

6. Stiggins, *Student-Centered Classroom Assessment,* 4.

Figure 1. Assessment Blueprint[a]

Purpose (why?):   Summative decision-making

Population (who?):   Grade 2

Target (what?):   Skills and techniques: *Read and notate music*

Benchmark: Demonstrate pitch direction by using visual representation MU.A.3.1.2

Competencies/Taxonomy:

    1.1   Demonstrate pitch direction through representative concrete drawing
        (skills, reasoning proficiency, products)

    1.2   Demonstrate pitch direction through body movement
        (skills, reasoning proficiency)

    1.3   Demonstrate pitch direction through the use of manipulatives
        (skills, reasoning proficiency)

Method (how?):   Performance (equal weight) 1.1–1.3

Conditions:

    Administration: Assessment may be administered in a large group setting with evaluator assessing individual performance.

    Time limits: Benchmark/competencies are assessed as part of instruction. Assessment can be administered in one class period.

    Materials: Recorded examples, paper, pencil, manipulatives

    Support during
      administration: None

Directions to Students:

1. The student will listen to the music and draw a picture to show the direction the melody moves. Shapes, lines, arrows, or other icons may be used to demonstrate the melodic direction.
and/or
2. The student will listen to the music and use the body (whole or part) to show the direction the melody moves.
and/or
3. The student will listen to the music and use the manipulatives provided to show the direction the melody moves. Blocks, bingo chips, craft sticks, etc., may be used to demonstrate the melodic direction.

Directions to Teachers:

1. Student should have prior experiences with this testing format.
2. The teacher will select 3–5 short music examples with contrasting melodic directions.
3. The teacher will select student performance mode (drawing, moving, manipulating objects), clarifying what the expectation is for each performance mode. Exemplars often aid in student understanding.
4. The teacher will review student directions and check for comprehension.
5. The teacher will review scoring criteria and check for comprehension.
6. The teacher will play music samples (multiple playings are allowed).
7. The teacher will use Analytical Rubric to assess student proficiency.

Scoring Specifications:

    Scoring Method: Analytic Rating Scale scored by certified music teacher

    Training: Certified music teacher

Other Specifications: Modifications for special populations must be considered. Clarify what accommodations might be allowed.

Figure 1, continued

Sample Assessment: The student will accurately demonstrate pitch direction using visual representation via concrete drawing and/or movement and/or manipulative objects. The following examples from *Share the Music, Grade 2*[b] will be used.

1. "Bow, Wow, Wow" (p. 302 CD6)
2. "Chinese Dance" from *The Nutcracker* (excerpt) by P. Tchaikovsky (p. 85 CD2)
3. "Hop Old Squirrel" (p. 143 CD3)
4. "Hot Cross Buns" (p. 300 CD6)
5. "Waltz of the Flowers" from *The Nutcracker* (excerpt) by P. Tchaikovsky (p. 85 CD2)

Analytic Rubric:

Criteria Rating Scale

0–1	2	3
Little or no understanding of the problem	Limited understanding of the problem	Full understanding of the problem
Accurate pitch direction is not observed in visual representation.	Accurate pitch direction is observed in part of visual representation.	Accurate pitch direction is observed in most or all of visual representation.

Criteria:

Demonstrate accurate pitch direction by using visual representation. A score of 0, 1, 2, or 3 will be marked for each example.

Music Examples:	A	B	C	D	E
• concrete drawing	___	___	___	___	___
• movement	___	___	___	___	___
• manipulating objects	___	___	___	___	___

Scoring code: Based on a total possible score of 15 (maximum 5 examples), with a scoring range of 0–15, a passing score of 13 will be used to determine student proficiency.

Grading Code: 13–15 = Performing successfully
8–12 = In the process of learning
0–7 = Improvement needed

[a] Adapted from M. Banerji, *Designing Alternative Assessment Tasks and Rubrics*, Workshop for Student Achievement Grant Educators, Pinellas County Schools, June, 1999.

[b]*Share the Music, Grade 2* software (New York: Macmillan/McGraw-Hill School Publishing, 1995).

7. Ibid.

8. Ibid.

9. Florida Department of Education. (1996). *The Arts*, 2.

10. Wiggins, G. (1992). Creating tests worth taking. *A Handbook for Student Performance Assessment in an Era of Restructuring*, 6 (2), 47–54.

11. Stiggins, *Student-Centered Classroom Assessment*.

12. Ibid.

Briana Foley is a music specialist for Garrison Jones Elementary School in Pinellas County, Florida. This article originally appeared in the September 1999 issue of Florida Music Director. *Reprinted by permission.*

Music: From a Performance Art to a Paper Test

by Maria Carroll Green

Little did I know the question, "Mrs. Green, may I see you in my office?" would be the turning point—the critical moment in changing my perspective on the way I teach my elementary vocal music classes. The question was posed by my principal, Dr. Lynn Jemmott. She wanted to submit my name for membership on the New Jersey Elementary School Proficiency Assessment (ESPA) Committee in Visual and Performing Arts. "Sure," I replied, acknowledging to myself that my chances of being accepted were equivalent to my winning a hundred million dollars. I submitted the necessary paperwork and quickly forgot the entire scenario. I was certainly surprised to be notified of my acceptance to "the committee"!

Finally, in 1997, the day arrived when I met the other members of the ESPA Visual and Performing Arts Assessment Committee. We were an eclectic band of dedicated and experienced art, dance, music and theater educators from various areas of the state. All of us were very passionate about our areas of expertise. Our goal was to design a valid assessment for visual and performing arts that mirrored the standards and allowed a district to monitor the progress. We were quickly inundated with a profusion of training that guided us through the sequential steps needed to create an assessment product. Our training included: goals of an assessment, types of assessment, development of an assessment, sensitivity training, creating a test plan, Bloom's Taxonomy, writing test items (selected response, and constructed short and extended response), writing performance exercises, rubric design, writing scripts and directions for assessments, writing task descriptions, weighing test items, creating a matrix, developing prototype items, and writing test specifications and statistics.

Fitting Square Pegs into Round Holes

You are probably asking, "How does all of the above relate to the here-and-now music classroom scene?" How does a square peg fit into a round hole?

I once believed that every minute of the music class period had to be filled with singing, playing instruments, creating, moving, reading or listening to music—a truly active and interactive environment. Student enjoyment was at its highest. The music period was fast-paced, high-energy and intense (something like an aerobics class). One senior teacher, with whom I worked during a summer program, warned me to allow the children to have some "downtime." This time allowed the children to reflect on the activities they had experienced. Needless to say, it took me quite a while to slow down (perhaps years of teaching had something to do with it).

As a result of participating on the committee and designing knowledge and skill statements based on the standards, I no longer try to teach everything I ever learned and hope to learn about music. I am more discriminating in what I teach and how I teach. I am more focused. Yes, less is more.

Presently, in my classes, we actually talk more. We discuss the elements of music, use appropriate music terminology, critique, analyze, compare, problem-solve, respond, and most importantly, make connections. The children are beginning to make the material their own. They have ownership of the concept and can now use it in another context. They are progressing to mastery.

How do I know? How can I assess their knowledge and skills with a written test?

Can It Be Taught in 25 Hours?

Let's address the content. What should a fourth-grade child know about music? What skills should a fourth-grade child possess to demonstrate that knowledge? Which pieces of knowledge and skills address the standards and CPI's (cumulative progress indicators)? How important is this material? Most importantly, what can be taught in approximately 25 hours of a year?

Students are familiar with the KWL Charts in their classrooms—"What I **K**now, What I **W**ant to Know, What I **L**earned." Let's use them in music. Use KWL Charts when introducing a song, unit, rhythm pattern or melodic pattern. This helps to focus the student on specific knowledge and skills.

Suppose the children are learning a new song from their songbooks. You may ask the children, "What do you know about this song?" Some possible answers may be, "It is written on a staff." "It has three verses." "There are mostly quarter notes." "The rhythm is repeated." "The melody goes up." "There are a half note and a half rest in the fourth measure." "There is a repeat sign at the end of the second staff." Symbols or terms that are not identified are placed in the "What I Want to Know" column.

Let's suppose you are studying ballads. Have the children create two lists: "What I Know about Ballads" and "What I Want to Know about Ballads." The majority of the "What I Want to Know" list may be, "What is a ballad?" That was easy—that's half of your lesson! After singing or listening to a ballad, the children might dramatize the song. Using terms from the theater, assign a director, a costume designer, a stage manager, scenery designer, and the like. Use the correct direction terms, such as, stage left, upstage, and downstage.

What did you want the children to know and learn from the lesson and activities? Children must know music terminology to be able to communicate what they know. I make a determined effort to write down responses of the children and terminology on the chalkboard. At the end of the day, my chalkboard is usually an array of words and music that only I can decipher.

Print-Rich Atmosphere

One way to facilitate learning music elements, music terminology and symbols (in addition to helping the visual learner, keeping sane, and saving arthritic fingers) is to make the room "print-rich." Posters on music terminology and symbols can be created on the computer. I usually use one sheet per term or symbol, with the symbol, name and definition on the sheet. With one item on each sheet, I can make the print large enough to be seen across the room. The sheets are laminated or placed in a plastic pocket and attached to the walls. Obviously, if you are a traveling musician, you may consider writing the information on a laminated chart that may be rolled up and carried from room to room. (I know it's not easy!)

When referring to a term or symbol, ask a child to point to the corresponding poster. The students can then add that information to the vocabulary or symbol section in their music folders. Folders help children to organize their work and to reflect on the material taught.

There are some drawbacks to having a "print-rich" atmosphere. All of your answers to the tests are on the walls. It took me a while to realize why some students in certain parts of the room were getting all of the questions correct. I was so proud of them. Now, I give tests with all of the "print-rich" materials proudly displayed on the walls. On a later date, I give the same test with the specific "print-rich" material covered. At least now the students know to read what is on the walls, and they know what they are looking for. (Yes, I'm devious.)

Pencil-and-Paper Assessment

You've completed your unit on the instruments of the orchestra. Now how can you assess what they have learned?

Model for your students how you would create a selective response question through a multiple-choice question or single-answer item. The parts of a multiple-choice question are: the stem (tells the student what is to be done), the distracters (the three incorrect choices), and the correct answer.

Develop a rubric for creating a good multiple-choice question with your students. A rubric is a scoring guide that identifies the expectations of the child at a highly competent level. It identifies what the child is expected to be able to do. Criteria should be listed in the rubric that account for varying levels and degrees of quality or competency.

Keep this rubric visible in the room, and direct the students to write the rubric in their notebooks. Now the fun begins—assign your students the task of developing multiple-choice questions.

When the questions are complete, students take center stage reading their multiple-choice questions. The remainder of the class listens and evaluates the question according to the rubrics. Afterwards, the students choose the correct answer. (Of course, one of the choices has to be the correct answer. Make sure that point is in your rubric.) You will have the pleasurable task of letting the students assess their knowledge. All you have to do is put the grade the students gave the presenter into your roll book. An example of a multiple-choice question is as follows: The trumpet is a member of the:

(A) percussion family.
(B) woodwind family.
(C) brass family.
(D) string family.

Ask the computer teacher for assistance in developing a multiple-choice quiz template. If you have a computer or a computer lab, let students type their multiple choice questions onto a disk. Voilà! You now have at least 20 different multiple-choice questions for twenty different assessments. Not only have you gained a little sanity, but your students are gaining mastery.

Another type of question calls for a "constructed response." In a constructed response question, the children are asked to write, draw, demonstrate, solve, or list. Examples of constructed response questions are listed below:

In "Peter and the Wolf" the composer chose French horns to represent the wolf. Give two reasons why you think the French horn was chosen.

List the names of the instrument families. Group the instruments shown in the pictures with the correct instrument family.

Choose an instrument and name its instrument family. What character or thing would you choose for that instrument to represent? Give three reasons why the instrument is a good choice.

A good rubric and response must display the student's knowledge of music elements, terminology, instruments, and instrument families. Students may address the timbre of the instrument, the pitch, the tone color, the mood, and dynamics that can be achieved on the instrument.

Why not establish a procedure of test taking 5 minutes before you trot off to your next class or 5 minutes into your class? Give a timed multiple-choice or constructed-response test from the multitude of student-made tests you have received. It might include a combination of question types representing various knowledge and skill components.

Good Assessment Provides a Range of Expression

Students may "show what they know" using various formats. The same concept, or piece of knowledge, may be presented from many different perspectives to accommodate multiple intelligences. Presentations of knowledge or skills may be in report form, collages, montages, dance, *Hyper Studio, Power Point,* a commercial, brochure, book, essay, poetry, graph, or musical composition. The possibilities are endless. Children present what they know in the learning style in which they feel the most comfortable. Don't forget the rubric for assessing the projects.

Moving with the Beat

Musicians are so creative and often move with the beat of the "teachable moment." Nevertheless, now that we are accountable for the students' learning, we must eventually move back to the standard being addressed. Let's not forego those "teachable moments;" just make sure the information is eventually covered. Keep a checklist of the standards, knowledge and skills taught. This task will be easier using the Test Directory and Specifications for the Visual and Performing Arts.

You and your students are now better equipped to use a performing art—music—as a catalyst for a great performance on a pencil-and-paper test.

Maria Carroll Green is general music teacher at Lincoln Elementary School in Englewood, New Jersey, and has served on the New Jersey Elementary School Proficiency Assessment Committee for Visual and Performing Arts. This article originally appeared in the May 2000 issue of New Jersey's Tempo. *Reprinted by permission.*

Assessment Tools for the Music Classroom

by Keitha Lucas Hamann

Systematic assessment is an often underutilized method for improving instruction in the music classroom. While informal assessment tools, such as observation, are used frequently to evaluate group progress toward a goal, more formal assessments that focus primarily on individual musical achievement are used less frequently. Though informal observations are useful in adjusting music instruction to address group weaknesses, it is only through formal assessment techniques that teachers are able to gather and report detailed, objective information regarding individual musical achievement.

Formal assessment of individual achievement in the music classroom is full of challenges. For example, formal assessment, particularly performance assessment, takes time. For the elementary general music teacher who may only see a class 30 to 60 minutes a week, testing is perceived to take away from valuable teaching time. Given the often hectic concert schedule, performance teachers may hesitate to reduce rehearsal time by giving tests.

A second challenge in using formal assessment is that music teachers sometimes have difficulty resolving the conflict between group learning and individual achievement. For performing groups where the emphasis is often on group rather than individual achievement, tests are perceived not only as interruptions to rehearsal time, but as irrelevant to group learning procedures.

The third challenge in using formalized music assessment involves the difficulty in defining musical skills such as tone, expression, or musicality. These are complex, interconnected skills that require the translation of aural concepts into written words. Because of the complexity of the tasks, it is difficult to create a measurement tool that is complete and yet adaptable to an infinite variety of sounds.

With all of the difficulties in utilizing systematic, individual assessment in the music classroom, why is it vital that music teachers make the effort to incorporate formal testing procedures into their classes and rehearsals? First of all, assessment results, such as grades and test scores, are the mechanism by which progress is communicated to others: parents/guardians, school officials, state agencies, and, of course, the students themselves. How the progress is measured communicates to these other people what is important in the music classroom. For example, when grades in performance ensembles are determined by attendance, attitude, or other nonmusical criteria, the message is sent that nonmusical criteria are more important than individual musical development in the music classroom. As music educators continue to struggle to validate music learning as basic to education, using musical criteria to grade and report progress in the music classroom becomes a very powerful communication tool.

As important as assessment is in communicating the results of musical learning, the single most important reason to use systematic assessment in the music classroom is to improve music instruction. When designed and used properly, results from specific performance and written tests can communicate to the teacher and to the individual student areas of musical learning that need improvement. This gives the student the opportunity to focus on specific learning deficits and to assume some responsibility for music learning. The teacher can use the detailed information from written and performance tests to tailor instruction to student needs, making music learning more efficient and appropriate.

To take advantage of formal assessment to improve instruction, music teachers have two different types of tests at their disposal. Written achievement tests may be used to determine student understanding of facts, dates, vocabulary, notation, listening skills, and/or composition skills. Performance achievement tests may be used to determine playing skill, musicality, sight-reading or sight-singing success, and/or other performance skills. Using written and performance assessments in combination allows music teachers to develop a more complete profile of student strengths and weaknesses that makes it possible for teachers to focus music instruction more efficiently.

While a detailed discussion of test design is outside the scope of this article, there are a few hints that can improve the reliability and validity of the information derived from music tests. The following are just a few of the ways that teacher-constructed tests can be designed for use in the music classroom.

Teacher-Constructed Test Formats

All testing is improved when teachers decide **before instruction** what is to be measured. By planning testing procedures in advance, the planning for instruction also becomes more focused, as learning objectives are addressed in a systematic fashion. There is nothing wrong with teaching to the test as long as the test is a good test that represents the content being taught.

A second key to improving overall testing is **balance.** Balance includes creating test questions to cover all instructional material in proportion to the amount of time spent on the instruction or the number of pages covered in a book. If, for example, two days are spent on dynamics and one day is spent on tempo vocabulary, the test for this material should have twice as many questions on dynamics as on tempo vocabulary. If three chapters in a book are covered and if the chapters are about the same length, then approximately one-third of the questions on the test should focus on each chapter.

Third, a well-designed test will address both **higher-level** and **lower-level thinking skills.** In addition to asking students to recall the number of beats a whole note gets, students should be asked to analyze, synthesize, and apply information in a variety of situations.

Finally, the test must be checked for **accuracy.** The correct answer should be clear, and incorrect choices should be plausible but clearly false. Humor and hints are to be avoided, as some stu-

dents will understand, but others won't. Definitions should be checked with a text, encyclopedia, or dictionary, and grammar and spelling should also be checked for accuracy.

Written achievement tests include both questions in which the answer is selected from given options, such as in multiple-choice, true-false, and matching questions, and questions that require the test taker to recall information, such as in completion, short-answer, and essay questions. One of the problems associated with questions in which students select an answer is the problem of guessing. The lower the chances of a student guessing the correct answer, the more reliable the information is. For example, a student has a 50/50 chance of guessing correctly on a true-false item but only a one-in-four chance of guessing correctly on a multiple-choice question. More reliable information allows for more accurate corrections during instruction because the increased consistency allows the teacher to trust the information received from the test.

There are several simple ways to minimize guessing on written tests. First, be careful to avoid grammatical clues such as "a," "an," and plurals. For multiple-choice tests, use a minimum of three answer choices. Keep all answer choices approximately the same length. Avoid "all of the above" and "none of the above" and absurd answers, as these give the test-wise student a better chance of guessing correctly. With true-false questions, consider having students correct or explain false questions in order to receive full credit. With matching questions, keep the number of answers larger than the number of questions or allow answers to be used more than once so that students don't guess the answer through the process of elimination.

Questions in which students must recall rather than select information make it harder for students to guess correctly. However, other problems may affect the reliability of completion, short-answer, and essay questions. In a completion question, the test taker supplies a word or words to fill in a blank in a sentence. To reduce the possibility of guessing the correct answer, grammatical clues should be avoided. Also, multiple correct answers should be minimized, and procedures should be in place to address misspellings and partial answers.

For both essay and short-answer questions, the questions must be specific as to what is expected in the answer. For example, "Discuss the symphonies of Mozart" leaves open a wide range of correct answers, while "Name three characteristics of form in Mozart symphonies" narrows the range of possible answers. In order to be more consistent in scoring an open-ended question, construct a sample answer in advance. Determine in advance how the item is to be scored, and be sure to let students know what the question is worth.

Reliability may also be a problem with performance assessments, as these assessments are inherently subjective. Music is an aural art. Performance assessment requires judges/teachers to evaluate the sounds created by the performer and to translate the assessment into numbers or words. Because the assessment is based on a judge's opinion, it is not possible for a performance assessment to be completely objective. However, steps can be taken in preparing a performance test that will make the test as objective as possible.

While performance assessment can focus on the entire performance (global) or on the elements within a performance (local), the more carefully the criteria are defined, the more reliable the test will be. As with written tests, criteria should be determined in advance, and students should be informed as to what the criteria will be.

There are several techniques, borrowed from psychology, that work well in clarifying criteria in a performance test. The first of these is the Likert-type scale in which the subject responds to a question by rating the answer on a scale between two extremes. For example, in responding to the statement, "This was an excellent performance," students would choose from strongly agree, agree, neutral, disagree, or strongly disagree. When the Likert-type scale is adapted for use in performance assessment, numbers might be used to represent each step on the scale (from 1 = strongly agree to 5 = strongly disagree or from 1 = excellent to 5 = poor). The more carefully "excellent" and "poor" are defined, the more consistent ratings will be.

Other performance measurements include a checklist in which the judge indicates successful completion of each task. Judges may also use a rubric that defines different levels of difficulty for a task. The student's score is the highest level successfully completed. For any performance measure, careful definition of the task is critical for consistent scoring. For example, good posture could include the following checklist: feet shoulder-width apart, knees flexed, shoulders back and down, hands to side, head centered, chin down. By checking off the elements that are completed, the teacher can let the student know what needs to be corrected.

Both performance and written tests are critical to improving instruction in the music classroom. Systematic use of tests gives teachers and students information to use in improving music learning. Basing assessments and grades on musical criteria communicates to parents and administrators the importance and validity of a music education. Taking the time to make sure that tests are balanced, accurate, and fair, results in more credibility for the music teacher. As formal assessments become more utilized, music programs are strengthened, and a strong credible program should be the goal of every music teacher.

Keitha Lucas Hamann is assistant professor of music education at the University of Minnesota in Minneapolis. This article originally appeared in the May–June 1999 issue of Ohio's Triad. *Reprinted by permission.*

Using Portfolios for Assessing Performing Ensemble

by Steven N. Kelly

It is possible that with the newly adopted *National Standards in the Arts* the use of testing may increase in American education. Subsequently, testing results could become a major force in shaping public attitudes about the quality of our schools, our school music programs and the capability of our students. Despite the potential growth of testing to demonstrate the effectiveness of the *Standards,* testing is a reported area that many music educators often do not understand well.[1] It is possible, that as music teachers, we are well trained in instructing students to acquire information, but not as well trained in strategies to adequately measure the effectiveness of our instruction and what our students are learning. Our failure to collect appropriate data on our teaching performance can mislead both teachers and students regarding the effectiveness of our music programs, possibly leaving our profession open to criticism as being too subjective in our evaluation methods.

Consequently, new testing methods are being developed which incorporate more direct assessment of student knowledge, performance and responsiveness. These methods could enrich the information provided by conventional testing methods by requiring students to create answers or products as a means of demonstrating what they have learned and how their experiences affected them. This method, sometimes called authentic assessment, often involves the student producing a portfolio of the work completed during a specific time period.

Authentic Assessment Using Portfolios

A portfolio is a collection of a student's work assembled over a period of time. Research has indicated that performance assessment is more reliable and valid if taken continuously over a long period of time.[2] The purpose of a musical portfolio is to provide a sample of a student's achievement and overall musical behavior and to gain indicators of program quality. Portfolio evaluations can demonstrate individual student learning processes, performance and the results of these actions. Portfolios can demonstrate how students receive and interpret information, generalize new information to previous knowledge and how students reorganize their mental structure to accommodate new understanding.

The portfolio's contents should reflect the student's best work and include required and optional material. For purposes of guidance and direction, it is suggested that specific criteria be established as an outline in formulating portfolios. Establishing the criteria can be based on program and school objectives, local and state educational objectives, the forthcoming *Nebraska K–12 Visual and Performing Arts Curriculum Frameworks,* or the *National Standards for Arts Education.* Table 1 lists examples of specific criteria which can be used in establishing a portfolio. Allowing students to assist in establishing the portfolio's content criteria is a positive way to include the student in the learning process. This activity will provide guidance to the student in formulating the portfolio and help to minimize subjectivity in the later evaluation.

Table 1. Examples of Specific Criteria for Establishing Portfolios

- Quality and variety of performances presented (tone, note accuracy, rhythm, intonation, expression)
- Quality, variety, and quantity of the performances attended
- Originality and creativeness of the material presented
- Depth of the material
- General use of correct language (grammar, punctuation, spelling, etc.)
- Aesthetic assessment
- Expressiveness of the material
- Material's scope (amount of different musical experiences presented)
- Student's self-assessment of the experience
- Allowances for individuality in style and viewpoints
- Ability to relate musical knowledge to other parts of the curriculum

There are many considerations which should be contemplated before making a final decision on the portfolio's contents. Among these are how much can be expected of the student's age level, what time length should the portfolio cover, and what process and criteria goes into the grading of the portfolio. Directors can increase direct student participation in the process by allowing students to comprise a list of portfolio content possibilities. This list can be used to make the final content selections (see table 2) and may include items reflecting a variety of musical styles, basic knowledge of history and theory, different performance situations including small ensembles and solo material, compositions, composer biographies, concert programs, or interviews of local musicians.

The time period students have to build their portfolios can range from a month to the entire school year. Due to the nature of most school settings, it is suggested that the portfolio encompass a semester in length. This time frame allows students opportunities to construct audiotapes, cover a variety of community musical events, and demonstrate significant progress in their individual performances.

Use of the Portfolios

Portfolios can be used by both teachers and the students in a variety of ways. The portfolio should reflect the student's best work and can be used to demonstrate problem-solving abilities, persistence,

sensitivity and creativity. Portfolios can help measure a higher order of thinking that often involves students performing in integrated environments. Colleges and universities often look for these characteristics in admitting students and awarding scholarships. Students wishing to major in music can use portfolios to help gain admission to music schools. Students can use portfolios as an introduction for themselves to music departments prior to their arrival on campus for auditions. For students wishing to go into the work field, the portfolio demonstrates characteristics which help in getting prospective employers' attention by setting these students apart from other applicants. Students can also use portfolios to gain entrance to summer music programs and qualify for these often limited scholarships.

Teachers can use portfolios to better evaluate individuals in their programs. Portfolios are excellent diagnostic tools which can be used to adjust instructional content to meet individual needs, as a basis for ability grouping and one method for providing accountability in music programs. The use of portfolios makes "teaching to the test" difficult due to the individualization. This factor may make this aspect of authentic assessment a more valid measure of teaching effectiveness. Perhaps the best use of portfolios by teachers is the ability to demonstrate creative thinking in music, which can be transferred to other areas. Teachers can

Table 2. Examples of Portfolio Contents

- Tape performances of solos, small ensembles (video or audio)
  1. a self-critique of the performance
  2. a short report on the compositions and why and how they were performed
- Tape performances of different musical styles (jazz, rock, classical, electronic, etc.)
- Outline of the compositions of 20th century orchestral composers
- Biographies of composers from different periods
- Examples of original compositions by the student
- Examples of computer-generated music program used or created by the student
- A theoretical analysis of a composition
- Programs or ticket stubs of concerts attended
- Reviews of music programs or compositions
- Interviews of local musicians
- New instrument designs

show that creative thinking in music is a definable and measurable entity which should not be confused with traditional music aptitude, performance achievement, general intelligence, or academic ability. Through this method, the importance of music experiences in our schools can be further justified and enhanced.

The portfolio results can easily be demonstrated to administrators, parents and community leaders. Not only can the material be used as a direct assessment, it can be used to directly demonstrate class activities, student progress and academic learning relating directly to other academic areas and vocational enrichment. As a result, the increased effective use of authentic assessment using portfolios may enhance music's position in our public schools!

Be Practical

While ideally the use of portfolios can help demonstrate more effective teaching and improved learning, the average music educator could have problems attending to the many requirements of this evaluation strategy. However, this does not mean that certain components cannot be used.

Scaled-down versions of portfolio assessments can be used for special activities in which only a small percentage of an ensemble would participate. These activities could include using portfolio evaluations to assess applicants for leadership positions such as drum major, section leaders, or ensemble officers. Portfolios could be used for students wishing to audition for select ensembles such as jazz band, show choir, or small ensembles. Such activities could still be based on established criteria and content. Though using a smaller version of the portfolio strategy, the ensemble director can still gain a much more direct assessment of a student's ability and knowledge, therefore making the required evaluation more reliable.

It is easy to assume that learning is occurring in the music classroom. While it is difficult to measure some aspects of musical learning, educators need to look for indicators of learning that can be used to alter and improve teaching strategies. While some music educators may believe that no grading system exists that adequately reflects what a student learns in the classroom, the use of portfolios through the process of authentic assessment may be an alternative technique that may indicate higher student performance and improve teaching effectiveness.

Notes

1. T. Clark Saunders, "The Assessment of Music Performance: Technique for Classroom and Rehearsal," Special Research Interest Group (SRIG) in Measurement and Evaluation Newsletter, no. 15 (Spring 1993): 7–10.

2. D. Wolf, "Opening Up Assessment," *Educational Leadership* 45 (November 1988): 24–29.

Steven N. Kelly is assistant professor of music education at Florida State University in Tallahassee. This article originally appeared in the August 1995 issue of Nebraska Music Educator. *Reprinted by permission.*

Assessment in the Music Class: Knowing What, How and How Much

by Cindy Kelsey

The band director begins class by announcing that playing tests will be the first activity of the day and that the members of the flute section will be first to perform. Roberta sits first chair in the flute section, so she knows that she will be the first person to perform this unexpected and undefined task. Her heart rate suddenly accelerates, she can feel her heart pounding, her hands begin sweating, and her mouth is extremely dry. The director announces the measure numbers in a particular piece that will be considered "the playing test," and everyone scrambles to find the passage. Roberta plays. When she finishes, the director picks up a pencil, raises one eyebrow, slowly and dramatically inhales, writes something in a book, then asks for the next flutist to play. Two days later, Roberta knows little about the outcome of the playing test except that she remains in first chair.

While this activity is one method a teacher could use to assess students' ability levels, the processes of assessment in schools today call for clearly defined and clearly communicated approaches. By employing a few instructional and assessment strategies, the playing test activity can have meaning for Roberta and support her musical growth, rather than being a mysterious experience. The main thrust behind assessment is that there are no surprises, no secrets, no wondering—each person is informed of and working toward attaining determined goals. Assessment is formally defined by Gronlund as the means and tools used to gather information about students and their achievements. The broad view of the process of assessment suggests great interaction among teachers and students. It is vital for educators to communicate the expectations of students and collaborate with students in the decisions related to students' future learnings.

Assessment involves knowing *what* students are expected to achieve, planning and implementing *how* students will reach the goals, and measuring the student's performance. This circular pattern of events and activities can be determined collaboratively with students, teacher and possibly parents. The plans can be changed, adjusted and redirected as needed with knowledge and agreement of the interested parties.

As we continue to develop understanding of assessment in the classroom, we will discuss the various aspects of the assessment framework: the "What?" (standards and curriculum), the "How?" (various assessment models), and the "How Much?" (how students are rated).

The "What?"

Determining what students should know and be able to do is the first step in implementing effective assessment in the music classroom. At the national level, MENC's 1994 publication, *National Standards for Arts Education,* outlines music standards as well as those for the other arts domains for grades K–4, 5–8 and 9–12. The Standards for each span of grades remains the same while the complexity of skills and understanding increases as one progresses through the levels. The Arts Standards were developed to be the national goals—statements of desired results—to provide a broad framework for state and local decision making.

The National Content Standards for music are:

1. Singing, alone and with others, a varied repertoire of music
2. Performing on instruments, alone and with others, a varied repertoire of music
3. Improvising melodies, variations, and accompaniments
4. Composing and arranging music within specified guidelines
5. Reading and notating music
6. Listening to, analyzing, and describing music
7. Evaluating music and music performances
8. Understanding relationships between music, the other arts, and disciplines outside the arts
9. Understanding music in relation to history and culture.[1]

Assessment plays an essential role in the learning that takes place in our music programs. The music curricula of a school district, and/or the learning standards that are mandated or advocated by governing bodies, articulate *what* will be learned and, therefore, *what* will be assessed.

The "How?"

Once standards are established and instruction is designed and delivered, the next step is to determine how students will be assessed. The traditional models of assessment such as multiple-choice and paper-and-pencil tests are useful in assessing some types of knowledge and skills, but more diverse models are required to assess production and performance, thinking skills and creative expression. There is growing interest in developing alternative assessment models, especially in the arts. One of the most popular forms of assessment emerging from the education reform movement is performance assessment, where students demonstrate arts-specific competence rather than generalized academic ability. The process portfolio is one means of documenting and assessing student thinking as well as other dimensions of artistic growth over time. The portfolio is an account of the student's artistic development, across time, that includes examples of the student's work from early drafts to final products. Such a model supports students' being more responsible for their learning, being reflective, and for assessing their learning, while the teacher primarily serves as the diagnostician or coach.

The key to quality assessment is a variety of assessment strategies to cover the range of musical learning demanded in the Standards. The strategies suggested below should be thought about when considering using the process portfolio with students. Videotapes and/or audiotapes are excellent ways of documenting students' creative activities and performances over time. Comprehensive holistic tasks and projects can involve students in a series of creative activities and performance opportunities as well as providing the possibility of critical analysis of musical works and performance while addressing their understanding of history and real-world applications. Students' observations and reflections can be recorded and compiled in journals, documenting what has been learned and how it was learned. Cooperative learning activities that involve students in learning concepts and then teaching them to others reveals much about their learning. Checklists of expectations involve judgments of student performance, behavior, or attitudes and can be based on direct observation by the teacher, students, parents or others. Finally, interviews and conferences with students will determine the depth of their understanding and give students a chance to reflect on their achievement.

While alternative assessment models may be considered much more relevant to arts assessment than the traditional means of assessing, many concerns are raised. Performance assessments usually are more time-consuming and costly to administer than multiple-choice tests. Issues related to reliability and validity of the assessments are often raised.

"How Much?"

When the question of "How Much?" is considered, two issues need to be addressed. First, if alternative and authentic assessment models are employed, how does one determine whether the student meets expectations? A scoring rubric, or scoring guide, is used for making scoring or rating decisions in alternative and authentic assessment activities. Much can be learned by reviewing scoring rubrics that accompany performance assessments from the state and national levels. Teachers who are involved in performance assessment need to understand how to construct rubrics to support their students' understandings and to be consistent in rating students. The construction of a rubric depends on the teaching or assessment purpose. Components of a rubric include: (1) scoring criteria; (2) levels of achievement; (3) descriptors; and (4) benchmarked examples for the levels of achievement.

The scoring criteria related to a rubric reflects what we expect students to know and be able to do and, therefore, what has been taught. The criteria are specific to the skills and understandings that students have been developing through classroom activities and homework. Students need to know the scoring criteria before they begin the assessment task. The assessment criteria should not be a surprise or a punishment.

The debate continues among educators related to the optimum number of levels of achievement that should be represented in rubrics. Some people believe that an even number of levels is preferred so that no one can choose the mid-point, while others say that 3-point or 6-point scales are best. The final answer lies in the purpose of assessment and the natural number of differentiations the task itself calls for.

Descriptors articulate the meaning of the levels 1, 2, 3, ... As descriptors are written, care should be taken to address similar criteria in each level.

Benchmarked examples for the levels of achievement are articulated for grades 4, 7 and 10 in the Washington state "Essential Learnings" for the arts. The benchmarks inform the users of skills and knowledge students should be working toward during a span of time. Districts may be expanding that model to create guidelines for each grade level.

Rubric development that systematically incorporates these components will support the reliability and validity issues that can otherwise be problematic in authentic and alternative assessments.

The second question to address is "How do we manage the data?" Changes in record keeping and management procedures may be in order. Teachers who are reporting success in this area are incorporating performance tasks into their instruction. Opportunities for sharing with colleagues and then developing new and better methods or adjusting current techniques of data management have been valued. Many teachers also report some changes in their patterns of record keeping and some indicate increased use of various technological tools. Several software packages are available for small portable computers such as Apple's *Newton* that allows the user to design the rubric as needed, then the user can carry the *Newton* easily in hand and record observations of students in real time. The data recorded on the *Newton* can be downloaded to an electronic grade book that exists on the user's main computer. Finally, keep using the techniques that you've developed and become skilled and confident in their use.

Conclusion

The nationwide call for educational accountability is demanding assessment that is relevant and meaningful. While music classes are often considered showcases for exemplary performance-based activity, the assessment of learning in music classrooms is not always clearly defined and implemented. First, learn what the learning expectations are for your students. Become skilled in designing instruction that focuses on the learning expectations and in using a variety of assessment techniques. Finally, develop valid and reliable methods of collecting data about students and explore possibilities of managing the information. While some teachers fear that assessment will take away the joy of music making for the Robertas in their classes, those who are successfully implementing a variety of assessment strategies are finding that the joy of music making is expanded and strengthened with concrete understanding and purpose reflected in elevated student achievement. Now is the time to take steps toward understanding more about and using good assessment techniques in the music classroom.

Note

1. Consortium of National Arts Education Associations, *National Standards for Arts Education* (Reston, VA: Music Educators National Conference, 1994): 26–29.

Cindy Kelsey, curriculum project manager for the Federal Way School District, is a doctoral student in music education at the University of Washington in Seattle. This article, which appears here in condensed form, originally appeared in the March 1998 issue of Washington's Voice. *Reprinted by permission.*

Kelsey **31**

Assessing Elementary Improvisation

by Carmen Lopez

The testing process is by no means a new phenomenon to the music teaching profession. As long as there have been music teachers, there have been evaluative judgments being made on students' musical behaviors. The effectiveness of those judgments, however, poses an interesting question. As music teachers, we tend to become comfortable with our methods of teaching and assessing and therefore fall into a "rut," adopting the attitude "if it ain't broke, don't fix it." Then somewhere in our quest for higher education we come across a course that challenges us to the very core by challenging the very methods we've grown so comfortable with. And now we're faced with a decision—we can ignore the constant stabbing to our conscience and just tell ourselves "this is the way we've always done it," or we can admit that there's always room for improvement and allow the challenge to lead us to finding more efficient and effective ways of assessing our students.

Assessment Can Be Informal and Formal

Assessment happens in many forms. The simplest and broadest form is the informal assessment, where some kind of evaluative judgment is made, such as, "that was very good." Most of us do this on a daily basis, often without even realizing we're doing it. There are also formal assessments, comprised of objective and subjective information used to make decisions relevant to our own music instruction as well as our students' music learning.

A good assessment should have several key elements:

- It should reflect the instructional activity, hence, measure what it's supposed to measure (validity).

- It should contain specific criteria used to measure the task at hand.
- It should provide sufficient data to make informed decisions about our students' progress.
- It should provide sufficient feedback to the students.

Subjective Judgments Are Most Difficult to Assess

While music teachers use both objective and subjective assessments, in my experience, it is those tasks that require subjective judgments that are the most difficult to assess. Tasks such as composition, improvisation, and performance are all complex tasks, which require complex assessment. We cannot fairly and effectively evaluate such a task based on one criterion, and that usually being our "musical expertise" as teachers and musicians. Therefore, we must develop criteria that communicate our goals and achievement standards.

I recently encountered this dilemma in my own classroom when I took on the task of teaching fourth graders the art of improvising on their recorders. The task was set up in question-and-answer form where the teacher played a two-measure musical question in 2/4 time using the allotted notes G-A-B-C-D and ending on the dominant "A," while the student had to answer with a two-measure phrase ending on the tonic "G." As they progressed, I realized I hadn't a clue as to how I was going to assess them. Sure, I could always listen and assign them a grade, as we are so apt to do. But why would this child get an A, while that one get a B? What were my criteria for evaluating this task? Could I explain to the students the difference between an A- and a B-performance? And was this really a fair and effective means of assessment? I quickly realized that the

Improvisation Assessment

Teacher _____ Grade _____

Assessment Categories	Poor (1)	Fair (2)	Good (3)	Excellent (4)
Executive Skills	• Uses incorrect posture and hand position • Consistently does not cover holes • Plays consistently too loud/soft • Slurs most or all of the notes together • Uses wrong notes or unknown fingerings	• Plays with correct posture or hand position • Covers some of the holes but leaves 2–3 holes uncovered • Plays with a good tone throughout but plays 2–4 notes too loud/soft • Uses combination of tonguing and slurring • Uses 2 wrong notes or unknown fingerings	• Generally plays with good posture and hand position • Covers most of the holes (misses one hole) • Plays with a good tone throughout but plays 1–2 notes too loud/soft • Tongues most of the notes • Fingers notes correctly, missing only 1 note	• Consistently plays with good posture and hand position • Consistently covers all the holes • Plays with a good tone throughout • Consistently begins each note with soft tongue • Consistently fingers all the notes correctly
Musical Skills	• Tempo varies greatly from that of teacher's musical question • Consistently cannot keep steady beat (too choppy or too many hesitations/stops) • Does not finish musical thought due to ending on the notes "A" or "C" • Requires 4 or more tries to complete response	• Tempo is a little faster/slower than teacher's musical question • Somewhat keeps steady tempo, making at least 2 rhythmic mistakes (i.e., hesitations/stops) • Student's answer completes musical thought by ending on "B" or "D" • Requires 3 tries to complete response	• Tempo is very close to that of teacher's musical question • Generally keeps steady tempo, making only 1 rhythmic mistake (i.e., hesitation/stop) • Student's answer completes musical thought by ending on "G" or "B" • Requires 2 tries to complete response	• Tempo matches exactly that of teacher's musical question • Plays consistently with steady tempo and rhythmic accuracy • Student's answer completes musical thought by ending on "G" • Requires only 1 try to complete response
Creativity	• Copies previous student's answer identically • Plays scale pattern (D-C-B-A-G) with no variation • Uses 1–2 notes in answer • Does not complete answer due to lack of effort	• Plays similar answer to that of prior student with minor rhythmic and tonal variation • Plays scale pattern (D-C-B-A-G) with slight rhythmic variation • Uses 3 notes in answer • Answer is longer than 2 full measures	• Answer is original and varies from previous student's answer • Plays scale pattern up or down but varies at least one tone • Uses 4 notes in answer • Answer is not complete due to leaving out last note	• Answer is original and greatly varies from previous student's answer • Does not play a scale pattern but combines notes and rhythms to form creative answer • Uses all 5 notes in answer • Completes answer in 2 full measures

main problem was the absence of criteria, and, in the absence of criteria, this classroom task was nothing more than an instructional activity. Criteria were necessary to help assess this complex task in a reliable, fair and valid manner.

Criteria Necessary for Assessing Improvisation

So I set out to develop criteria for assessing this improvisation activity. This led to the development of a rubric (see sidebar) which was nothing more than setting up criteria in different categories.

While the development of criteria requires more effort up front on the part of the teacher, it certainly makes assessment much easier in the long run. Because improvising is a complex task comprised of playing an instrument, demonstrating musical skills, and creativity, those became the three categories in my rubric. The skills required to produce a good sound on the recorder were labeled "Executive Skills." "Musical Skills" encompassed mostly the rhythmic aspect of their performance, while the "creativity" category assessed their ability to improvise an answer. In each category, criteria were established which defined achievement standards ranging from excellent to poor. For each category, I found it easiest to characterize an "excellent" performance first, then move to the extreme and characterize a "poor" performance. The two gradations in between, the "good" and "fair" performances, required a little more thought. However, at the conclusion there were specific criteria that not only guided my judgment in assessing their performance, but it would also make public to the students the standards for these judgments. Once this task was complete, a transparency was made, and before beginning the assessment process, it was reviewed with the students so there would be no question as to how they would be graded. The only thing left to do was to use the rubric.

Results Reveal Teacher Bias

The results were surprising. Not only did I have to go back and make a few minor adjustments to the rubric, but two striking realities leapt out. The first was the realization that teacher bias does enter into our judgment even among the most nonbiased teachers (if such a thing exists). Because all the students were being judged using the same criteria, there was no room for teacher bias. The second was the fact that, void of criteria, we really cannot make reliable, fair and valid judgments. The use of the rubric allowed me to grade the different aspects of their performance individually, pointing out their strengths and weaknesses, while not punishing their entire performance because of one area of weakness (which is what happens when we judge a complex task using only one criteria).

Sharing with Other Teachers

The final step in the development of the rubric was to let other music teachers use it to test for reliability. Using taped samples of my students, three other elementary music teachers were asked to assess the same students using the same criteria. The findings showed the reliability was indeed satisfactory for classroom use.

The development of criteria, in this case in the form of a rubric, is vital for tasks requiring subjective forms of assessment. It not only helps make the evaluations more objective, but it also enables the teacher to define "excellence" to the students and help them achieve it, while also providing students with concrete feedback on their performance. Above all, it helps the teacher be accurate, unbiased, and consistent in assessing student performance. Personally, this was a growing process, which required me to move beyond my comfort zone to come up with more effective ways to assess and, therefore, help my students. After all, we demand and expect them to give us their very best. How can we do any less for them?

Carmen Lopez teaches in Dade County Public Schools in Florida. This article originally appeared in the September 1999 issue of Florida Music Director. *Reprinted by permission.*

Performance-Based Assessment and Increased Student Performance

by Gina May

Simply put, assessment is about defining standards—it is about making human judgments.

We make judgments constantly about all aspects of our lives. As teachers, we make continual judgments about students; judgments are about criteria whether we articulate them or not. Our choice is either to make the criteria clear or keep everyone guessing.

There are at least three types of criteria:

Product — performance, project, etc.
Process — efforts, participation, etc.
Progress — how far the learner has come.

Using only one type of criteria for judgment is a problem; using all three criteria to devise a single judgment also has undesirable effects. Balance these three types of criteria in ways that:

1. support student motivation to learn.
2. identify what a student has learned and can do as a result of instruction.
3. consistently communicate developmentally-appropriate standards of excellence.
4. inform instruction strategies and methodologies.
5. make teacher and students collaborative partners in the learning process, which is an important aspect of making performance-based assessment work.

In the absence of an articulated public assessment criteria, we are left with inferences, guessing games, sliding standards, and a focus on "Is that what you wanted?" "Is this right?" "How am I doing?" "Does this count?" We also increase the potential for not focusing on what really matters and what is really important in the learning domain. The danger of doing "activities" in the hope that students are learning something and acquiring skills abounds. In addition, the issue of personality conflicts can easily serve as a focal point or excuse for nonachievement.

Here is a "quickie" checklist of questions and "to do's" when beginning the process of establishing assessment criteria:

1. Describe the attributes that illustrate the skill or behavior in question.
2. Write descriptions and definitions of those attributes, not what a good performance looks like.
3. Cluster the attributes and define traits or dimensions with examples.
4. Generate descriptions of strong, middle, and weak performances on each trait. Use adjectives and descriptive phrases. Use samples of student work. Identify the developmentally-appropriate range of performance—the beginner, intermediate, and accomplished. These are often referred to as benchmarks.
5. Develop a scoring scale to rate each trait. These are numerical, qualitative, or both.
6. Try it out—revise, refine, modify. Include students in the process.
7. Make the criteria "public." Use them as a learning tool.

Ambiguous or unstated criteria distances the learner from real learning and from taking responsibility for learning. It can lead to fuzzy and biased decision making about student grades, and it can mean that important time is spent on unimportant activities. The arduous and difficult up-front task of developing performance-based assessent criteria pays off by focusing on increased student achievement and improving instruction.

Involve students in any portion of the process when you feel comfortable doing so.

Gina May is state supervisor of visual and performing arts/assessment at the Office of the Superintendent of Public Instruction in Olympia, Washington. This article originally appeared in the January 1997 issue of Washington's Voice. *Reprinted by permission.*

Assessment Tools for Kindergarten and First-Grade General Music Students

by Martha Snell Miller

In 1983, when I began teaching elementary general music, the course of study I used had a column for evaluation. Many objectives for each grade level indicated evaluation should occur through teacher observation of student performance. I began to wonder if I had the ability to validly observe hundreds of students. Remembering many things about many students was possible. However, I could not recall enough about every child to answer questions about their musical progress. Actually, at times I had trouble recalling a grade level or mental picture of a particular student. To compound the problem, only fifth- and sixth-grade students received achievement grades for music class. For those students, I always recorded observations and scores from any written work and gave each student points for his or her nonmusical classroom behaviors. However, my record-keeping was minimal for the younger children who did not receive report-card grades in music.

New Ideas

In 1994 the elementary music teachers in my school district began writing a new curriculum for our general music students. We soon recognized that determining the extent to which our students accomplished the goals of our curriculum needed other procedures beyond teacher observation. We not only wanted to assess students who receive music grades, but also those who do not receive a report-card grade. Because of limited amounts of time and heavy schedules, we decided to start in a small way. We simply could not take on all of our students in one year! We decided to start at the beginning (a very good place to start) with first grade. We were unable to choose kindergarten because all of the elementary music teachers do not teach kindergarten music classes. Fortunately, the administration supported our efforts as long as each of the three elementary teachers agreed to use the same assessment procedures.

Looking at Other Examples

A search for examples of assessment procedures and tools already in use for elementary general students provided few examples. However, many articles suggested good assessment tools for large musical ensembles. Some criteria from those examples seemed to be relevant for general music as well. Several of the articles indicated that the first step is to determine what criteria we want to assess. Some of the examples were assessed in four categories: cognitive, psychomotor, affective and nonmusic criteria.[1] Our own outcomes identified for first graders seemed to fit well in the psychomotor domain, particularly in relation to performance. In deciding what to include in the portfolios, we consulted the Mitchell Robinson article on alternative assessment techniques. He indicates that portfolios may include authentic assessment examples such as audiotapes or journals and traditional assessments such as standardized tests, or aptitude and achievement tests.[2] One of the outcomes in our curriculum was that each student would be able to identify and use his or her singing voice within a limited range. We decided that a recording of each student singing would be the best way to determine each child's progress. Each student's voice could be effectively measured through the use of the Singing Voice Development Measure, which has been used in research experiments with many students in this district.[3] The author gave instructions to the other music teachers, and we set off labeling a tape for each of our first graders and making a recording of their singing voices. The children were more than happy to sing into our microphones (not one student refused), as each privately took his or her turn at a special job of recording his or her singing voice. When we told the students we would be adding these to a portfolio for each of them, one excited student said, "Oh, we have portfolios in our other subjects!" Another voice chimed in with, "Maybe we could have a portfolio night and allow our parents to hear us sing!"

Including an aptitude score for every first-grade student became our next step. After completing the tonal and rhythm tests of Edwin Gordon's Intermediate Measures of Music audiation, each student received a tonal and rhythm score which was recorded on a student aptitude profile card. Each first-grade student now has a large manila envelope, labeled with his or her name, that contains a tape of his or her singing voice achievement and tonal and rhythm aptitude scores for the first-grade year. We hope to continue adding assessment measures to this portfolio. In future years, students' voices will be recorded again, and aptitude scores for each year will be recorded.

Lessons We Learned
After we made portfolios for one grade level, we all agreed that starting small was a great idea. However, even though we thought we were starting small, the project became very time-consuming. The author felt that the secretarial task of making these portfolios was especially time-consuming. Typing labels for each tape, correcting aptitude tests, making a card for each student, and putting the portfolios away in alphabetical order consumed many hours. Each elementary music teacher did individual testing with the student while a substitute taught our music classes for a day. However, I can certainly say that if I have a question about the skills of any first-grade student, I now have an objective source to provide answers.

Future Activities
After one successful adventure, I have decided to try another. Because I teach all of the kindergarten students in the entire school district, I decided to create an assessment tool that would be usable for all of my kindergarten students. I wanted to create something that the student could see, add to a future portfolio, and copy and send home to parents as a kind of music report card. Once again, I started by deciding what kinds of musical behaviors I wanted from my students and how I could best measure those. My creation looks like the chart in table 1, and I plan to use it in the following way. Students will have their own card posted in my room on cupboard doors or bulletin boards. As each student achieves the musical behaviors shown in the left-hand column, they take a rubber stamp and place a musical symbol in the column to the right. Each stamp shows the sign of successful completion of that objective. This means students keep the records that are always visible to the whole class. Later this chart becomes part of a portfolio, and a copy can be viewed by parents. I am quite sure kindergarten children will love seeing their own card fill up with stamps and be proud of their achievements.

Other Ideas
Many future ideas using these portfolios are under consideration. We have discussed ideas like hosting a portfolio night and inviting parents to hear a recording of their child's singing voice achievement and to review the aptitude scores their children received over a three-year period. Perhaps an instrumental teacher could look at the portfolios of the fifth-grade beginning band students to better meet the needs of those students.

An Example to Follow?
Assessment of musical goals has begun in our district, and hopefully we can continue and learn more. Taking one year at a time and biting off just what we can chew has been an exciting activity for the elementary music teachers in our district. Perhaps you could design simple tools for your elementary students. Remember to start with something you think you can handle, assess the objectives stated in your curriculum, and look at the examples of others.

Notes
1. Mary Ellen Junda, "Grading Students in Performing Groups" (Research Update), CMEA News (December 1992): 14–15.

2. Mitchell Robinson, "Alternative Assessment Techniques For Teachers," Music Educators Journal 81, no. 5 (March 1995): 28–34.

Table 1. Kindergarten Assessment Chart

Name _____ **Class** _____

I can use my singing, speaking, whispering, and calling voices.		
I can sing a song with my class.		
I can sing a song with a small group of students.		
I can sing alone while the class listens.		
I can sing the part of the Tingalayo alone.		
I can sing the answers to the animal song alone.		
I can find and keep a steady beat with my hands and my feet.		
I can play a steady beat on an instrument while my class sings.		
My class can sing one part of a song while my teacher sings another.		
I can sing one part of a song while my teachers sings another.		
I can find the big beats and the little beats and show them with my hands.		

3. Joanne Rutkowski and Martha Snell Miller, *The Effect of Teacher Feedback and Modeling on First Graders' Use of Singing Voice and Developmental Music Aptitude*, Symposium on Research in General Music, University of Arizona, Tucson, AZ, February 1995.

Martha Snell Miller is general music teacher at the Foot of Ten Elementary School in the Hollidaysburg Area School District in Duncansville, Pennsylvania. This article originally appeared in the November 1995 issue of Pennsylvania's PMEA News. Reprinted by permission.

Assessment— Applying the Yardstick to Musical Growth

by Glenn E. Nierman

In my early years I can remember how important it was for me to grow taller. After all, how could I be a decisive force on the basketball court unless I was at least as tall as Wilt Chamberlain?! [For all of you nonbasketball fans or fans familiar with more recent basketball heroes, Wilt Chamberlain was a seven-foot center for the Kansas Jayhawks in the late 1950s.] I would get the yardstick out of the hall closet at least once a week to see how much I had grown. It was important for me to **assess** my progress toward a goal that I had established for myself.

Today we also hear much about **assessment**. It all seems so complicated; terms like *authentic assessment, performance assessment, portfolios,* and *rubrics* have replaced older, more familiar descriptors such as *tests* and *measurement*. I'm not sure what all of the "hoopla" is about. Just as I used the yardstick to measure growth, so assessment, regardless of whatever descriptor modifies it, calls on the educator to measure growth. Has the student made progress in moving from point A to point B? Has growth occurred in the student's skill development or knowledge base? Has his or her attitude changed as a result of instruction?

I have decided to devote several articles to understanding **performance assessment** and what it implies for the music educator. Performance assessment does not sound unfamiliar to most of us. We have been involved in a type of performance assessment at the secondary level through contests for a number of years. Contest ratings do provide us with some useful information; but as an assessment tool, contests are far

from valid and reliable. How can *growth* be assessed on the basis of a "one-shot" measurement?

Expanding Our View through Understanding Key Features

Performance assessment, as used in educational circles today, has a much broader definition with more far-reaching implications. One succinct, yet insightful, definition of performance assessment is:

> testing that requires a student to create an answer or a product that demonstrates his or her knowledge or skills. (Office of Technology Assessment, 1992, p. 1)

A wide variety of assessment techniques can be harbored within this broad definition, such as projects, interviews/oral presentations, demonstrations and portfolios.

One key feature of performance assessment, *active participation,* is a feature which we as music educators could utilize more often. Rather than simply choosing from presented options such as are required of music students when they are told that they will be required to play/sing one of three given excerpts from the music they have been rehearsing, students could be asked to create a rhythmic warm-up using the characteristic rhythms in one of those particular passages, for example. This allows for a demonstration of not only mastery of the passage and the understanding of distinctive rhythmic features, but it provides a vehicle for a creative product which is uniquely the student's work of art. The research literature tells us that not only would this activity probably provide the motivation to complete the task, but it also has the potential to increase the retention of the rhythmic features so that they could be applied to other musical situations more easily.

A second key feature of performance assessment is that such assessments require students to *demonstrate* knowledge or skills; therefore, the process by which they solve problems becomes important. To illustrate, students could simply be asked to perform rhythm patterns noted in several meters which had been projected on the screen. Perhaps a better demonstration of their understanding would be to ask them to create rhythm patterns in several different meters using any combination of several given rhythmic values. Now when the students perform their metered examples, the teacher has a better insight into the process by which the students tried to solve the musical problem. Remember, these patterns do not have to be long or complex. It was Jerome Bruner who said that any subject can be taught to any child at any time at any stage of development in some "intellectually honest form."

Thirdly, performance assessment items should *directly reflect intended outcomes.* Whereas a traditional test might ask students to list the rules for finding the high point or most important note of a phrase, a performance assessment would ask students to demonstrate their understanding of phrase molding by editing the dynamic markings of several different passages. A traditional test might ask students to match key signatures with home tones; a performance assessment may ask them to create a new scale and then to write the scale from at least one other tone.

Finally, Rudner and Boston (1994) point out that "performance assessment can also measure skills that have not traditionally been measured in large groups of students—skills such as integrating knowledge across disciplines, contributing to the work of a group and developing a plan of action when confronted with a novel situation" (p. 4). Try asking students to organize an event such as a Renaissance Fair. You might be surprised what they could demonstrate about the music, literature and science discoveries of the time period.

Is Performance Assessment Just Another Bandwagon?

Certainly performance assessment has been in the news lately. It has been the subject of a number of books and articles. Entire issues of major education journals, including *Educational Leadership* (April 1989 and May 1992) and *Phi Delta Kappan* (February 1993) have been devoted to performance assessment. Our own music education profession is in the middle of designing an entire plan for the National Assessment of Educational Progress (NAEP) based on performance assessment principles.

It is also true that there are a number of dimensions of performance assessment that are not new. Good classroom teachers have used projects and portfolios for years. They have designed activities that involve students in blending skills and insights across disciplines.

Regardless of whether performance assessment is new and in the news or whether it is a reworking of concepts from the past, I do not believe that it is just another bandwagon. The performance assessment is more than just a few "new" measurement techniques (rubrics, portfolios) or applying technology to assessment. It requires identifying the skills and concepts we want students to master and empowering teachers to make decisions about appropriate goals and objectives for individual students. Indeed, it requires examining the very purposes of education. Now that performance assessment has been described and its key features identified, future articles can describe various performance assessments, weigh their advantages and disadvantages as instructional tools and accountability measures, and offer suggestions to music educators who want to use performance assessment to improve teaching and learning.

References

Office of Technology Assessment, Congress of the United States. (1992). *Testing in American schools: Asking the right questions.* Washington, DC: Government Printing Office.

Ruder, L. M., & Boston, C. (1994). Performance assessment. *The ERIC Review, 3* (1), 2–12.

Glenn E. Nierman is interim associate director and professor and chair of the music education division at the University of Nebraska in Lincoln, as well as chair of the Nebraska Coalition for Music Education. This article originally appeared in the August 1996 issue of Nebraska Music Educator. *Reprinted by permission.*

Criteria for Evaluating Performance Assessment

by Glenn E. Nierman

The educational community at large is currently undergoing much criticism regarding how achievement is measured in the classroom (Haney and Madaus, 1989; Fuentes, 1994). To date, music education has, for the most part, remained aloof to this criticism, for various reasons. One disturbing reason for this aloofness is that some music educators feel they put their students "to the test" before the public, often in the form of performances for community groups, contest judges, etc. Therefore, they are already engaged in **performance assessment**; the growing dissatisfaction with testing in the schools, therefore, does not apply to music education.

I believe that this view is somewhat shortsided. Yes, there is a certain amount of *group assessment* that can occur in performing situations; but, the *National Standards for Arts Education* (1994) calls upon us to assess the skills and knowledge of the *individual* student with respect to the discipline of music. This responsibility should be taken very seriously. Music is now in the core of the curriculum, and we must be able to assess individual growth in music just as we assess individual growth in math, science and English. We must be able to converse with parents about their child's progress or lack of progress in music just as classroom teachers and teachers in other core subjects talk about achievement in their respective disciplines.

It is not enough to meet this challenge by simply vowing to give at least one "pencil-and-paper" test and/or to use one standardized test in music so that there will be some "objective" information to discuss with parents. If this is all we do, we fall prey to the same criticisms which have been leveled against education in general. Critics charge that standardized tests and multiple-choice tests, which are assessment tools that have been used heavily in the past,

- give false information about the status of learning in the nation's schools.
- are unfair to (or biased against) some kinds of students (e.g., minority students, those with limited proficiency in English, females and students from low-income families).
- tend to corrupt the processes of teaching and learning, often reducing teaching to mere preparation for testing.
- focus time, energy and attention on the simpler skills that are easily tested and away from higher-order thinking skills and creative endeavors—the Achilles' heel of the nation's education system today, in the view of many observers (Haney & Madaus, 1994, p. 684).

Judging the Effectiveness of Assessment Tools

All this is not to say that standardized tests or multiple-choice tests have outlived their usefulness and should not be used in the music classroom. These tools can be a valuable part of an assessment package, but they should not comprise the total package. Like other educators, however, we in music education must be engaged in a search for alternatives to testing. **Performance assessment**, broadly defined by the Office of Technology Assessment (1992) as "testing that requires a student to create an answer or a product that demonstrates his or her knowledge or skills" (p. 1), seems to offer a variety of assessment techniques—projects, interviews/oral presentations, demonstrations and portfolios—all worthy of our exploration. However, whether assessment techniques used in the music classroom include standardized tests or some alternative, what is needed is a critical attitude toward assessment techniques. It is the purpose of this article to continue a focus on performance assessment by proposing several criteria for judging performance assessment techniques to be introduced and explained in future articles. I would like to suggest that the following four criteria will serve well in evaluating any assessment techniques: validity and reliability; intellectual honesty; fairness; and ease of administration.

Validity and Reliability

As with any test, assessment alternatives must be valid and reliable. If an assessment is *valid,* it, quite simply, measures what it is supposed to measure. For example, if you are interested in measuring a student's skill in reading certain rhythms and you devise a 16-measure phrase containing the rhythms that were supposed to be mastered in the key of g-flat minor, you will probably not get a *valid* assessment of the student's rhythmic reading skill because this unfamiliar key will not allow the student to focus on the rhythms. You are assessing the student's familiarity with g-flat minor. A more *valid* measure of rhythmic reading skill could be designed by asking the student to sight-read the 16 measures with the rhythm only notated on a single pitch.

Reliability is a matter of *consistency.* Do the results you might have obtained from the assessment differ from week to week, from day to day, because of the nature of the assessment? Does the structure of the tasks themselves cause students' performance to be inconsistent? If so, the task is probably not as reliable as it could be.

Intellectual Honesty

This criterion is based on Jerome Bruner's statement that any subject can be taught to any child at any stage of development in some *intellectually honest* form. Intellectual honesty is important because it is an important key to transfer. To help clarify, consider this example. A music educator who decides to assess students' understanding of quarter and eighth notes in a duple meter by asking the students to chant the note name "quar-ter, quar-ter, eighth, eighth" when reading a rhythmic pattern is not using a method that is as *intellectually honest* as a teacher who asks students to perform the task using nonsense syllables such as "ta" and "tee tee," because the word "quarter" is a two-syllable symbol being used for

a single beat duration. "Ta" is more intellectually honest because it can later be more easily transferred to more conventional rhythmic reading systems.

Fairness

Just as validity, reliability and intellectual honesty are imporant criteria to be used in judging assessment tools, so fairness seems to be crucial, too. Questions to be asked are: Do scoring practices reflect students' capabilities fairly? How will I use and interpret the results of the assessment?

Utilizing performance-based assessment tools raises concern that the performance tasks chosen and the scoring procedures used be appropriate for all students taking the assessment. Students in our classrooms have diverse backgrounds and experiences. Disparities exist between students due to differences in their familiarity with, and exposure to, various assessment tools and in their motivation to perform and learn. Miller-Jones (1989) suggests that teachers use "functionally equivalent tasks specific to the culture and instructional context of the individual being assessed." Stiggins (1987) suggests that in order to score students fairly, it is crucial that the scoring procedures used ensure that the "performance ratings reflect the examinee's true capabilities and are not a function of the perceptions and biases of the persons evaluating the performance."

Ease of Administration

Finally, when time and money are limited, the practicality of the assessment procedures are important. Generally, performance-based assessments are more time-consuming and costly than more traditional alternatives, especially when large numbers of students (such as music educators teach) are involved. The costs may be justified, however, if performance-based assessments are going to significantly affect the ways teachers teach and students learn.

Where Do We Go from Here?

Now that several criteria for judging performance-based assessment tools have been explained, teachers who want to implement performance assessment need to think critically about what alternatives are best for their music students. The time for change is now. If music is a "core" subject and essential for all students, then we must assess musical growth with the same rigor as other subjects that have traditionally been considered to be "in the core of the curriculum."

References

Consortium of National Arts Education Associations. (1994). *National standards for arts education.* Reston, VA: MENC.

Fuentes, E. (1994). Standards, assessments, and the national education goals. *The ERIC Review, 3* (1), 17.

Haney, W., & Madaus, G. (1989, May). Searching for alternatives to standardized tests: Whys, whats, and whithers. *Phi Delta Kappan,* 683–87.

Miller-Jones, D. (1989). Culture and testing. *American Psychologist, 44* (2), 360–66.

Office of Technology Assessment, Congress of the United States. (1992). *Testing in American schools: Asking the right questions.* Washington, DC: Government Printing Office.

Stiggins, R. (1987). NCME instructional design and development of performance assessments. *Educational Measurement: Issues and Practice, 6* (3), 33–42.

Glenn E. Nierman is interim associate director and professor and chair of the music education division at the University of Nebraska in Lincoln, as well as chair of the Nebraska Coalition for Music Education. This article, which appears here in abridged form, originally appeared in the October 1996 issue of Nebraska Music Educator. *Reprinted by permission.*

Tools for Assessing Musical Skills

by Glenn E. Nierman

Performance assessment could be succinctly defined as "testing that requires a student to create an answer or a product that demonstrates his or her knowledge or skills" (Office of Technology Assessment, 1992, p. 1). In music, authentic assessment tasks fall more within the "skills" category than the "knowledge" category because the skills required to make music are far more a psychomotor activity than a cognitive one. Unfortunately, skill development has not been considered a basic part of schooling, or at least it has not been considered on a par with cognitive development. Bloom (1956) himself commented that "we find so little done about [skill development] in secondary schools or colleges, that we do not believe the development of a classification of [skill] objectives would be very useful at the present" (pp. 7–8).

Recently we find that skill development seems to have been somewhat elevated in its status in the hierarchy of school goals. This is primarily the result of physical education personnel who convinced educators and decision makers that students did not need to be stars on a football, basketball, or volleyball team to derive benefits from skill development in physical education. Physical education was deemed necessary for *all students.* Likewise in the *National Standards for Arts Education* and our *Nebraska K–12 Curriculum Frameworks in the Visual and Performing Arts* we speak of the mission of arts education in Nebraska as providing "comprehensive arts experiences to empower *all students* [italics added] to enrich their understanding of themselves and the world" (*Nebraska Curriculum Frameworks,* 1995, p. 3).

In music education at all levels—elementary, middle school, high school, college—where group performance has so long been the focus, teachers are beginning to understand that they have an obligation to *all students* in their classes to monitor individual growth in musical skills. It cannot be overemphasized that incidental, cursory observations made in terms of sections, ensembles, or classes often lead to invalid assessments that hinder rather than aid the learning process. How many times haven't we heard or made comments such as: "My second graders can't match pitch;" "The flutes are continually flat;" or "The tenors' tone quality is thin and breathy above the staff"? The teachers who limit their assessments to these kinds of observations have demonstrated that they are not concerned about individual skill development, but production of the best total effect. Performance assessments must be made in terms of the individual's growth rather than group progress. If the individual's skill-level improves, so will the level of the group.

Individual assessment in music is not an easy task. We deal with large numbers of students who are often different in age and different in terms of their musical skill development. In order to accomplish individual skills assessment, some tools or aids that are uniform for all students must be used. Assessment tools that seem to hold a great deal of promise for individual skill assessment in music are checklists, numerical rating scales and graphic rating scales or rubrics.

Checklists

Perhaps the most common performance assessment tool is the checklist. The list may be used for any type of skill evaluation and can contain whatever features the teacher feels to be desirable for that skill. Secondary teachers are typically familiar with checklists since contest rating forms are really a type of checklist. Preparing a checklist is perhaps as valuable as using it because you become aware of the importance of sequence and the relationship among the checklist items. To prepare a checklist, simply identify the competencies or outcomes that are to be observed; a simple checkmark placed beside an item could indicate achievement of the desired outcome/competency.

For example, a fifth-grade general/vocal music teacher might want to assess his or her students' ability to sight-read four-measure phrases using a mallet instrument. The assessment checklist for this skill might look like the checklist in figure 1.

Applying the assessment criteria of validity and reliability, intellectual honesty, fairness and ease of administration (for further information on these criteria, see Nierman's article "Criteria for Evaluating Performance Assessment" in this book), the checklist seems to be a viable assessment alternative. It certainly is easy to administer, and, by applying the same criteria to everyone, there is a "built-in" sense of fairness. The checklist seems to call attention to the very essence of sight-reading using a mallet instrument. Therefore, it is, to some degree, valid. Reliability, that is, consistency, might be questioned, however, when listening to a number of students over a long period of time.

Rating Scales

Rating scales add a second dimension to the simple checklist: they allow the teacher to report not only if the competency/outcome has been achieved, but the quality or degree to which it has been achieved. Rating scales are of two primary types—*numerical rating scales* and *graphic rating scales.*

When using a *numerical rating scale,* the teacher constructs a series of outcome/competency statements as with the checklist, but the numerical rating scale allows the teacher to make a judgment not only about the achievement of the outcome/competency, but also the quality or degree to which it was achieved by placing a mark on a numerical scale or continuum whose extreme limits have been defined by the teacher.

The competencies/outcomes used in the checklist example might be modified to utilize the numerical rating scale format as shown in figure 1. With this format the teacher communicates more detailed feedback to the student.

The *graphic rating scale* is very similar to the numerical rating scale. Again the teacher has the opportunity to denote the quality or degree of achievement on a continuum with the extreme limits being defined. However, with the graphic rating scale all points on the continuum are defined by verbal descriptors instead of numbers

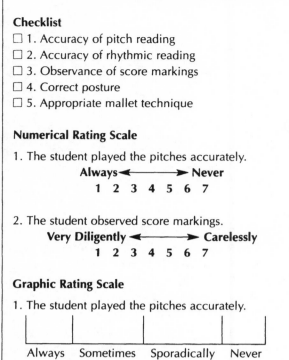

Figure 1. Examples of Checklists and Numerical and Graphic Rating Scales

Checklist
☐ 1. Accuracy of pitch reading
☐ 2. Accuracy of rhythmic reading
☐ 3. Observance of score markings
☐ 4. Correct posture
☐ 5. Appropriate mallet technique

Numerical Rating Scale

1. The student played the pitches accurately.
Always ◄——————► Never
1 2 3 4 5 6 7

2. The student observed score markings.
Very Diligently ◄——————► Carelessly
1 2 3 4 5 6 7

Graphic Rating Scale

1. The student played the pitches accurately.

| | | | |
Always   Sometimes   Sporadically   Never

(see figure 1). Notice that the major difference between the graphic and the numerical rating scales is one of format. Do you want to give feedback to students based on numbers or verbal descriptors? The numerical rating scale is somewhat easier to construct. Sometimes it is difficult to find appropriate verbal descriptors for all points on the continuum.

Rubrics

Unlike the checklist and the rating scales previously described, the word *rubric* is a relatively unfamiliar term to many music educators. A rubric, simply put, is a form of graphic rating scale. For example, when you are asked to complete a reference form for a student teacher or colleague, graphic rating scales (rubrics) are often used to report your assessment of the applicant's capabilities with respect to certain criteria deemed essential for good teachers. There may be items on such a form that define specific "criteria," such as, "How would you describe the applicant's general health and pattern of attendance?" Then, you may be asked to place a checkmark in certain "standards" categories related to the criterion, such as, "Vigorous & Healthy; Never Absent," "Excellent; Rarely Absent," "Good; Prompt & Regular in Attendance," or "Fragile; Frequently Absent or

Tardy." Rubrics that are used for assessment in the classroom are simply a series similar to criteria and standards statements in which certain criteria describing what students should know and be able to do are stated and certain standards describing various levels of performance for each criterion are listed.

When designing rubrics for the classroom, it may be helpful to use a rubric grid like the one shown in figure 2. In developing rubrics, the following sequence is suggested:

1. Decide what criteria are related to a performance objective.
2. List the criteria in the vertical column of the rubric grid.
3. Visualize what a learner would be doing when meeting each criterion listed in step 2 in an exemplary manner (advanced level).
4. For each criterion, begin writing the advanced level indicators (what does the exemplary performance look like?) by identifying the key behaviors to be demonstrated by the students.
5. Record the key behaviors identified in step 4 in sentence form in the first vertical column of the grid.
6. Repeat steps 3 through 5 for each level of indicators (standards) needed for the assessment.

The fifth-grade general music assessment task, when put in the rubric design, might look something like the rubric in figure 3. Notice the similarities between the graphic rating scale and the rubric. In both, the outcomes/competencies or criteria are defined. The difference is that instead

Figure 2. Sample Rubric Grid

	Standards		
Criteria			

of using several evaluative descriptors to denote quality or degree of achievement, a short description of what the learner is doing when he or she performs at a certain level is given. This description has less subjective connotations and should increase the reliability of the assessment.

Summary

The comment is sometimes made that musical learning cannot be clinically approached in the manner suggested by these assessment tools. Yes, there are some factors, such as describing what the student is doing when he or she sings or plays with "good tone quality," that are difficult to assess. How do we find the right words to assess this very subjective dimension? We haven't even been able to agree as a profession on what constitutes "good tone quality"! Nevertheless, a subject that belongs in the core of the curriculum and has been declared by law to be in the core of the curriculum must be accountable for what it purports to teach. I believe that our efforts to assess individual musical skill development can only result in

Figure 3. Sample Fifth-Grade Rubric Design			
Criteria	**Standard 1:** **Needs Improvement**	**Standard 2:** **Developing**	**Standard 3:** **Acceptable**
1. The student played the pitches accurately.	Most pitches are inaccurate; it is difficult to find the steady beat.	Some pitches are missed; usually only the more difficult, such as large intervals or unusual skips.	Most pitches are accurate; student continues playing within the beat structure even when an occasional pitch error occurs.
2. The student played the rhythms accurately.	[Description of student performances at "standard" level]		

moving us closer to being accepted as belonging in the core of the curriculum.

Author's Note. For more information about checklist, rating scale, and rubric construction, you may want to access the following items:

Boyle, J. D., & Radocy, R. (1987). *Measurement and evaluation of musical experiences.* New York: Schirmer Books.

Gregory, C. (1994). The tool you need for assessing writing [Writing workshop]. *Instructor, 104* (4), 52–54.

References

Bloom, B. (Ed.). (1956). *Taxonomy of educational objectives, Handbook I: Cognitive domain.* New York: David McKay Co., Inc.

Consortium of National Arts Education Associations. (1994). *National standards for arts education.* Reston, VA: MENC.

Nebraska Department of Education. (1995). *Nebraska K–12 curriculum frameworks in the visual and performing arts.* Lincoln, NE: Author.

Office of Technology Assessment, Congress of the United States. (1992). *Testing in American schools: Asking the right questions.* Washington, DC: Government Printing Office.

Glenn E. Nierman is interim associate director and professor and chair of the music education division at the University of Nebraska in Lincoln, as well as chair of the Nebraska Coalition for Music Education. This article, which appears here in slightly abridged form, originally appeared in the February 1997 issue of Nebraska Music Educator. *Reprinted by permission.*

Can Portfolios Be Practical for Performance Assessment?

by Glenn E. Nierman

In preivous articles, I have focused on performance assessment, i.e., "testing that requires a student to create an answer or a product that demonstrates his or her knowledge or skills" (Office of Technology Assessment, 1992, p.1). A wide variety of assessment techniques and products can be harbored within this broad definition, such as playing/singing tests, composition projects, interviews/oral presentations, demonstrations and portfolios. Portfolios will be explained in this article, and their practicality for music settings will be examined.

How Do Portfolios Relate to Assessment?

One meaning of *portfolio* is simply that the term refers to a portable case for carrying papers or drawings. In fact, long before portfolios were suggested as being useful for assessment, visual artists were carrying portfolios of their drawings to prospective employers. I have a friend who now works for Hallmark in Kansas City who told me about the care that he took to select the drawings that were part of his Hallmark interview portfolio. He wanted the portfolio to demonstrate that he was a current, active artist; he wanted it to showcase his skills and artistic knowledge; and he wanted the portfolio to show his growth as an artist. It seems to me that it was no accident that over a decade ago Lee Shulman and others in the field of education saw the portfolio, a collection of student products and "diaries" about the process of learning, as a viable assessment tool. The criteria that my friend had for his portfolio sound remarkably similar to several key features of performance assessment: active participation, authentic demonstration of skills/knowledge and direct reflections of growth.

One key feature of performance assessment, *active participation,* is a feature that we as music educators could utilize more often. Rather than simply choosing from presented options such as are required of music students when they are told that they will be required to play/sing one of three given excerpts from the music that they have been rehearsing, students could be asked to create a rhythmic warm-up using the characteristic rhythms in one of those particular passages, for example. This allows for a demonstration of not only mastery of the passage and the understanding of distinctive rhythmic features, but it provides a vehicle for a creative product that is uniquely the student's work of art. The research literature tells us that not only would this activity probably provide the motivation to complete the task, but it also has the potential to increase the retention of the rhythmic features so that they could be applied to other musical situations more easily. This "rhythmic composition," in its written, notated form or recorded on audiocassette, would make an excellent portfolio item.

A second key feature of performance assessment is that such assessments require students to *demonstrate* knowledge or skills; therefore, the process by which they solve problems becomes important. To illustrate, students could simply be asked to perform rhythm patterns noted in several meters that had been projected on the screen. Perhaps a better demonstration of their understanding would be to ask them to create rhythm patterns in several different meters using any combination of several given rhythmic values. Now, when the students perform their metered examples, the teacher has a better insight into the process by which the students tried to solve the musical problem. Remember, these patterns do not have to be long or complex. It was Jerome Bruner who said that any subject can be taught to any child at any time at any stage of development in some "intellectually honest form." With an item such as this in the student's portfolio, the teacher has a definite "springboard" to facilitate more learning about rhythm.

Finally, and perhaps most importantly, portfolios enable teachers to document *growth*. One of the criticisms of traditional methods of testing is that they are too product-oriented. Yes, traditional assessment tools, such as the multiple-choice tests about the musical features of a work, give us a picture of what the student has learned. That one measure, when used alone, however, cannot tell us anything about the growth in knowledge that has occurred. A more authentic way of assessing growth (and an excellent item for a portfolio) might involve asking students to write a letter to a friend before and after studying a musical work that you are rehearsing, explaining why the friend should or shouldn't purchase a CD of the musical work.

What Other Components Might a Musical Portfolio Contain?

Below are some additional suggestions for items that could be part of a musical portfolio:

Personal Growth Plan. If one of the features of performance assessment is the measurement of growth, then it seems important that the student and the teacher work together in developing goals and objectives for the student's musical development before instruction begins.

Practice Record. Why not include documentation of the individual's effort in enhancing his or her musical skills?

Audiotapes. What an excellent tool to document growth!

Concert Critique Forms. These will give the teacher and the parent some insight as to the criteria students are developing for making judgments about the music in their world.

Creativity Project. The *National Standards for Arts Education* implore us to not only guide students in the re-creation, but in the creation, of music. Perhaps students could be asked to notate the melody of a pop song for their instrument and then write a variation on this melody.

Student Self-Evaluation Forms. It is important to know what your students are thinking about their abilities as musicians.

Teacher Critique Forms. It is also important for your students to know your assessment of their musical abilities.

Listening Assessment. Again, the National Standards suggest that we should develop musicians with discerning, discriminating ears!

Lists of Musical Accomplishments. Why not use the portfolio as a database for musical honors such as All-State participation, honor choir membership, etc.? Students applying for scholarships will appreciate a complete record of their achievements.

Student's Value Statement. Decisions are made based on value systems. It is important for students to reflect on the value of music in their lives. Perhaps pose a question like this one to students: "If I couldn't be in choir next year, ... ?"

There are no limits to the amount and kinds of items that a musical portfolio might contain, but be wary of the "pile it higher and deeper" syndrome. Make the portfolio a realistic and useful tool. Why not involve the students in deciding what they want their portfolios to contain?

Why Use Portfolios for Assessment?

There are advantages and disadvantages to portfolio assessment. Two of the most frequently-voiced concerns involve time and storage space. How will I ever have time to file and read all of this material? Where will I store the students' portfolios? The classroom teacher only has to keep a portfolio for twenty-five to thirty students. How can this be done for several hundred music students?

The answer is—involve the students themselves in creating and storing their portfolios. A major advantage of using the portfolio for assessment is that it provides an opportunity to make students accountable for documenting growth in musical skills and knowledge. Other advantages of using portfolio assessment are:

Documentation of "Real World" Experiences

What will students be doing with music after they finish with their school music experiences? Yes, we hope that they will continue to sing or play an instrument, but they will all be consumers of music. What listening skills have they developed? What criteria will they use to make judgments about the music they encounter? The portfolio can help students to grow in areas other than performance-skill development.

Meeting Individual Needs

Music offers *all students* the chance to be successful. With portfolio assessment, goals and objectives can be altered to meet an individual student's musical needs.

Documentation for Conferences

This may seem like a very practical matter, but it is nonetheless important. Portfolio assessment provides concrete material to discuss with parents or administrators concerned with students' growth and progress.

Epilogue

Will portfolios, a form of performance assessment, be utilized by music educators in the months and years ahead? The answer to this question seems difficult to predict at the present time. In my view, any tool that requires us as teachers to identify the skills and concepts we want students to master and empowers us to make decisions about appropriate goals and objectives for individual students is worthy of serious consideration.

References

Consortium of National Arts Education Associations. (1994). *National Standards for Arts Education.* Reston, VA: MENC.

Office of Technology Assessment, Congress of the United States. (1992). *Testing in American schools: Asking the right questions.* Washington, DC: Government Printing Office.

Glenn E. Nierman is interim associate director and professor and chair of the music education division at the University of Nebraska in Lincoln, as well as chair of the Nebraska Coalition for Music Education. This article originally appeared in the April 1997 issue of Nebraska Music Educator. *Reprinted by permission.*

Creating, Performing, and Responding in Music: A Look at the Nation's Report Card

by Glenn E. Nierman

The NAEP Music Assessment was designed in conjunction with the voluntary *National Standards for Arts Education* (Music Educators National Conference, 1994). For the NAEP assessment, the nine content standards for music were essentially grouped into three general themes in the NAEP framework:

- creating (including content standards involving composing, arranging, and improvising)
- responding (incorporating content standards such as analyzing and evaluating music and performances, listening with understanding, and demonstrating knowledge of music in relation to the other arts and to history and culture)
- performing (singing or playing instruments).

Creating tasks used in the NAEP assessment gave eighth graders the chance to create a rhythmic improvisation, create a harmonic improvisation, create an embellishment on a familiar tune and use improvisation to create an original melody. Students were asked to play familiar tunes by ear on a MIDI keyboard or to sing familiar tunes when provided with an accompaniment to demonstrate their performing abilities. Students who were enrolled in music activities in school or out of school were also asked to perform by sight-reading a short melody, practicing and performing an excerpt of a large ensemble piece for their instrument or voice and evaluating their work. The eighth-grade students also were asked to demonstrate their ability to respond to music by analyzing and describing aspects of music they heard; critiquing instrumental and vocal performances; displaying their knowledge of music notation, and presenting evidence of their knowledge of the role of music in society.

Relationships between Background Variables and Performing Scores

In an attempt to determine the relationship between the amount of time spent participating in various activities that are part of in-school music classes (listening, singing, and playing instruments) and students' NAEP music performing scores, Persky, Sandene, and Askew, authors of the *NAEP 1997 Arts Assessment Report Card,* report the following:

> … sampling estimates of the total percentage of eighth-grade students not enrolled in a music class ranged from 34 to 40 percent. This group of students obtained a total of from 27 to 29 percent of the total possible points available for performance items. (1998, p. 38)

Perhaps a reason for this strong showing is that some of these students participated in out-of-school music activities.

On the other hand, students who reported that they sang "almost every day" or "once or twice a week" in music class scored in the range of 36 to 40 percent of the total possible points for performance. Students who played instruments "almost every day" or "once or twice a week" obtained a total of 38 to 53 percent of the total possible performance points. It is not surprising that students who have an opportunity to practice music performance skills and to receive feedback about their performances from music specialists would "perform" markedly better on the NAEP performing test. Those teachers who are working to help their students achieve National Music Standards one and two (singing and playing instruments) are making a difference in their students' performing skills.

Relationships between Background Variables and Creating Scores

It should come as no surprise that not many music teachers ask students to write music or to make up their own music in school music classes. The NAEP assessment shows that 36 percent of the sample who had music in the curriculum "never or hardly ever" were asked to write music, and 47 percent who had music classes in school "never or hardly ever" were asked to make up their own music. These two activities (writing music and composing music) did not seem to make a great difference in students' NAEP creating scores, however. Students who reported participating in these two activities "almost every day" only received two percent more of the total possible points on the NAEP creating assessment than students who "never or hardly ever" were engaged in writing or composing music. Playing instruments did seem to make the greatest difference in students creating scores, increasing the percent of the total possible points available for performance items from 31 percent for those who reported that they "never or hardly ever" play instruments to 50 percent for students who reported that they played "almost every day" (Persky, Sandene, & Askew, 1998, p. 39).

This is a curious relationship. Apparently playing instruments is more effective in promoting higher creating scores than asking students to "make up their own music." Perhaps this is a result of teachers' lack of knowledge about how to teach composition effectively.

The Effect of Out-of-School Variables

Only 11 percent of students tested reported taking private lessons on a musical instrument or in singing; however, this activity increased the total percentage of points received in the NAEP performing subtest from 31 to 59 percent of the total performing points and from 32 to 52 percent of the total creating points. This is a significant

increase. Similarly, listening to a musical tape, CD, or record produced marked increases in both performing and creating scores (Persky, Sandene, & Askew, 1998, p. 41). (It should be noted that 92 percent of the sample reported that they listened to musical tapes, CDs, or records.)

Again, it is not surprising that private lessons and out-of-school listening improves students' performing ability. However, it is noteworthy that these activities also improved creating scores. The effect of various in- and out-of-school music activities on students' creative music ability is certainly worthy of further investigation.

Summary

It is beyond the scope of this article to present detailed information on the relationship of background variables and students' NAEP responding scores, but "students whose responding scores were in the upper level of the scale reported significantly higher rates of participation than students in the lower level of the scale for many in-school and out-of-school music activities" (Persky, Sandene, & Askew, 1998, p. 44).

What will be the effect of "The Nation's Report Card" for music education? Will our profession be "promoted" to continue in the 21st century curriculum? Are there assessment practices utilized in this examination that you could use in your classroom?

References

Consortium of National Arts Education Associations. (1994). *National Standards for Arts Education.* Reston, VA: MENC.

Persky, H., Sandene, B., & Askew, J. (1998). *The NAEP 1997 report card: Eighth-grade findings from the National Assessment of Educational Progress.* Washington, DC: U.S. Department of Education. Available on-line (http://nces.ed.gov/naep/report97/1999486.shtml).

Glenn E. Nierman is interim associate director and professor and chair of the music education division at the University of Nebraska in Lincoln, as well as chair of the Nebraska Coalition for Music Education. This article, which appears here in condensed form, originally appeared as "Creating, Performing, and Responding in Music: A Look at the Nation's Report Card in Music—Part 4: Context" in the October 1999 issue of Nebraska Music Educator. Reprinted by permission.

Arts Education Assessment: The Journey and the Destination

by Frank S. Philip

Assessment in arts education has made a quantum leap over the past ten years and yet many goals of this recent explosion of activity are still shimmering on the horizon. This article describes the current landscape of arts assessments in the states and examines some critical educational, social, political, and economic challenges along the path to improvement.

There are perhaps two principal arguments for assessing arts education achievement in our schools; one for sound educational reasons, and one that addresses more crass dimensions of reality. But whether sacred or profane, both should be addressed by arts educators.

The first reason is the most important and the true intent for student assessment. Thoughtful, well-constructed and administered assessments provide important information about the learning process to a variety of stakeholders. Sound assessments furnish valid and reliable evidence for determining whether instructional expectations are being met.

Second, all assessments play a role in defining what is important in schools and contribute to shaping policy decisions about what happens in schools. These decisions are also being driven by student assessment results that are used for teacher, principal, school, and district accountability purposes. Because education is governed by political, economic, and social forces beyond the classroom, assessments can convey a deeper message about what is perceived to be important in our culture and plays a role in establishing larger priorities in our society.

Assessment As Information about Learning

There is little argument about the importance of student assessment in education. Well-crafted assessments can provide significant evidence of instructional effectiveness and student learning. Assessments provide a way to match the intentions for learning (the curriculum) with the delivery of experiences and activities for learning (the instruction). The results inform the learner, the teacher, the parents and the community about levels of student achievement toward expected goals and establish feedback in the system by providing information about the need for modifications in the instructional program. The entire learning process benefits from consistency between what is taught, how it is taught, and what is assessed.

Good assessments should account for different learning styles of students. They should be sensitive to the way assessment materials are introduced and the way appropriate response modes in the language of the art form are provided. They should replicate authentic instructional activity, and expect students to construct meaning from the knowledge and skills learned in the instructional program.

Rather than fragmenting the educational experience into meaningless facts, figures, and disconnected actions, good assessments should reflect the holistic nature of the learning experience and engage students in activities where they can demonstrate and apply their knowledge and skill and in practical and authentic assessment exercises.

These types of experiences are commonplace in curriculum-embedded assessment activities in the arts classroom, but infinitely more difficult to achieve in large-scale, on-demand assessments. Therefore, a comprehensive arts assessment system should employ multiple measures to construct a more complete picture of achievement from the National Assessment of Educational Progress (NAEP) at the national level through state assessments that are conceptually linked to local and ongoing classroom assessments employing portfolio and other measures over time. No single arts assessment should be expected to cover all learning expectations or all the legitimate uses of the assessment results.

Assessment's Role in Decision Making

Over the past 20 years, student assessment results have become an increasing part of education accountability systems. To many decision-makers, the test score provides apparent proof of the effectiveness of the curriculum, schools, principals, and teachers. This growing reliance on tests has been matched by higher stakes or consequences for good or poor performance.

The rationale goes something like this: we spend a lot of money on education and we want to make sure our money is well spent. One measure of success is the scores of students on tests. If we make higher test scores a criterion for success and reward or punish students and schools on the basis of those scores, we can induce excellence in the educational system.

But there are a few faulty assumptions about using student assessments in high-stakes applications. Many tests used for high-stakes accountability are assumed to represent an appropriate sample of the broad spectrum of educational experience being assessed. Another assumption is that they represent irrefutable evidence of that learning. Most often, they are neither and usually only measure a small slice of the expected content and often a kind of learning that is associated with memorization of facts.

By increasing the stakes, the answers on the test become the object of teaching and learning. The tail wags the dog, and the curriculum is narrowed to the confines of the content of the assessment. This constriction often impinges on the time for arts instruction by applying a priority system that moves aside "less critical" subjects in favor of those found on the high stakes assessment. It seems that what is most important to the public is tested, and what is tested becomes what is taught.

No single assessment can account for the myriad of factors that influence the educational achievement of students. Properly used, they only provide a piece of the evidence. Unless the arts are part of the assessment and accountability system, administrators and parents will not want to spend time and other precious resources on them.

Arts education faces another complex challenge. Like any other subject, the arts need to demonstrate effective teaching and student achievement, but all too often they must also convince the public and school administrators of the important role the arts play in a good education. Assessment has a role to play in both.

Generally, most arts educators have had little experience in developing arts assessments. As long as we were on the margin of education, we could be complacent about assessing student achievement. Assessment may have been appropriate for the left-brained subjects but not the fragile, ephemeral, "hard to measure what I do," arts. But when the arts became part of the national Goals and the National Assessment of Educational Progress (NAEP), it was necessary and important to come to the table with more than vague promises about what an arts education means. The arts education field needed to come to consensus on a well-defined vision of what it means to be arts literate and a process for determining when a person has achieved those expectations.

In the past decade, Goals 2000, the presence of National Standards for Arts Education, and the National Assessment of Educational Progress (NAEP) Arts Assessment have been powerful engines for change and, at the same time, created a positive effect on the public's perceptions about art education. Who thinks arts education is important? None other than our Uncle Sam himself!

Inclusion as a "basic" in the National Goals for education provided authorization for development and federal funding. The National Standards demonstrated high and rigorous expectations for arts education content, arguing that the experiences and knowledge found in arts education have a role in everyone's life, not just the talented few. The NAEP demonstrated that the arts could be assessed using innovative, performance-based methods that employed new technology to gather the evidence and scoring systems that were sensitive to the arts forms. They also created new ways of reporting the results with a CD-ROM that captured the sound and sights of the assessment.

But even with these advances, arts education still faces formidable and historically nonsupportive public opinion and perceptions about the nature and value of arts education. And for many people, perceptions are reality. According to the various Gallup polls on education over the years, the public places arts education in the lowest priority of all the subjects in school. This pervasive marginalization of arts education, together with a tradition of programs in the schools that only deal with talent, performance, or creative expression, has produced a society with a jaundiced view of the importance of arts education.

The problem is not that the public is against arts education. The dilemma seems to be a case of benign neglect, a result of the public's inadequate perceptions about the value of sequential arts education experiences. Without sufficient information and experience, the personal belief systems that generate the public's priorities in local schools are unable to support the types of programming many educators and citizens feel is absolutely essential to develop a knowledgeable, thoughtful, sensitive, questioning, innovative, and creative society.

But the problem is not only with public perceptions. The high expectations found in the National Standards and measured in the NAEP are not often apparent in the instructional programs found in most arts classrooms. Many arts teachers need to catch up with the latest developments in standards-based education and student assessment. To quote the old Pogo cartoon, "We have met the enemy, and he is us."

Fortunately, the rich and transforming experiences embedded in assessment development make the journey along the path to improvement as important as reaching the destination. The process of developing an assessment in arts education is a first-class education in aligning the intended curriculum with what is taught, how it is taught, and how achievement is assessed—a process that underscores the old adage: "When the potter shapes the clay, the clay shapes the potter."

Sitting down with a group of fellow teachers to discuss a scoring guide for student work produces more "ah-ha's" than just about any other professional development experience for educators. While defining content, examining clarity in instruction, determining acceptable evidence of student achievement, and voicing a wide range of other issues, teachers bring to the surface and discuss epiphanies, revelations, and personal insights that become a powerful common vision and consensus on what constitutes a good arts education.

Benefits can be realized by the entire arts education profession when we as arts educators can be clear and consistent about the intentions of a good arts education program and when that message can be clearly communicated. When the public becomes aware of the message and the message becomes common knowledge, the public's perceptions will change and arts education will become a higher priority.

A History of Recent Arts Education Assessment

At the beginning of the final decade of the 20th century, the convergence of increased regard for arts education and increased interest in new forms of student assessment produced new opportunities for arts education assessment.

In order to take advantage of these opportunities, the arts education profession needed to find the best path to travel. However, the history of large-scale assessment in arts education in America would make a thin guidebook indeed. But the landscape did feature some significant landmarks and early pathfinders. At the national level, the pioneering effort that began in 1969 on the new National Assessment of Educational Progress in the arts provided a path for us to follow.

On the arts side, leaders like Paul Lehman in music and Brent Wilson in visual art worked with Ed Roeber and other psychometricians on the test-development side to produce two sets of forward-looking NAEP assessments for art and music in 1973–74 and 1977–78.

These assessments featured some performance measures as well as the more traditional selected-response formats (multiple-choice, true-false, and matching). But like the current NAEP, the scope of the assessment was limited by budget concerns, and the results were not produced in a timely fashion. Unfortunately, the outcomes of the 1970 NAEP efforts made little impact on the arts education field or on education in general.

But the history of arts education assessment is not confined to the NAEP efforts. Over the years, many states have supported efforts to create large-scale assessments in the arts. Today, thirteen states currently have either assessments being conducted or have plans on the books for assessing the arts. The Large-Scale Arts Assessment in the States chart (see sidebar) provides a profile of that activity.

One state, New York, has a history of assessing its prescribed high school curricula in the arts as part of the Regent's system. For example, on Thursday, June 23, 1955, from 1:15 to 4:15 only, the University of the State of New York provided

Large-Scale Arts Assessment in the United States

	Disciplines	Grades	Purpose(s)	Sample	Status	Item Type (%)	How Administered	State Education or Arts Agency Contact	Comments
IL	D,M,T,V	4,7,10	2,4,5	Matrix Sample of all students	In Place	Selected Response (100)	Component of general assessment	Judy Dawson (ED) 217-782-4823	Based on state mandate; arts are one of the six basic areas of learning. Ten arts questions are in the same test as social studies questions. Through matrix sampling, different sets of questions are randomly distibuted among students.
KY	D,M,T,V,L	5,8,11	4,5	School Reports	In Place	Selected Response (33) Extended Response (67)	Component of general assessment	Jimmie Dee Kelly (ED) 502-564-2106	Extended response scores impact a school's accountability index. State Index devotes 5% to arts at elementary level and 7.5% at middle school and high school level.
MA	L	3,4,7,8,10	1,2,3,4,5	All Students	In Place		Component of general assessment	Susan Wheltle (ED) 781-388-3300	Literature is assessed as part of English/ Language arts. Other disciplines may eventually be assessed at local levels (based on state-developed standards).
MD	D,M,T,V	TBD	2,3,4,5	TBD	In Planning	TBD	TBD	Jay Tucker (ED) 410-767-0352	Task force working toward building arts assessment. Contractor for assessment development identified in Summer 1999.
ME	D,M,T,V	4,8,11	2,5	Matrix Sample	In Place	Selected Response (30) Short Answer and Extended Response (70)	Component of general assessment	David Cadigan (ED) 207-287-5807	The standards adopted by the state make the visual and performing arts a "basic" part of Maine's *Learning Results* standards and assessment program.
MN	D,M,T,V,L	9–12	1,3,5	All Students	In Place	Range of Evidence Accepted	Administered at classroom level	Pam Paulson (ED) 612-591-4708	Minnesota Board of Ed. has adopted graduation examinations in Reading, Math, and Writing. The state has adopted 10 additional areas of learning that include the arts. Students are required to create and/or perform in the arts and are assessed at the classroom level using a site-developed rubric.
MO	D,M,T,V	3 grade levels	2,5	TBA	Voluntary 2000, Required 2001	Selected Response Extended Response (% TBA)	Stand alone assessment	Larry Peeno (ED) 573-751-2857	Arts were not designated as a core subject area by the legislature, but the State Board of Education has designated them as part of the core, and assessment is being funded as a result of that designation.
NJ	D,M,T,V	5,8,11	1,2,3,4,5	All Students	Oct. 2001	Selected Response and Short Constructed Response	Stand alone assessment	Dottie Bennett (ED) 609-984-4568	New Jersey has also added an interdisciplinary component to measure more complex cognitive behavior at higher thinking levels.
NY	D,M,T,V	9–12	1,2,3,4,5	All Students	2001	Selected Response (25) Performance (75)	Stand alone assessment	Roger Hyndman (ED) 518-474-5922	Plans for high school graduation requirement.
OK	M,V	5,8,11	2,5	All Students	Field Test 97–98 In Place 98–99	Selected Response (100)		Paulette Black (Arts) 405-521-2931	Part of Priority Academic Student Skills.
PA	D,M,T,V	4,7,10	2,5	TBA	Piloting	Selected Response (30) Performance (70)	TBA	Beth Cornell (ED) 717-787-5317	Developed as part of Federal grant. Will eventually be used as a model for classroom-level assessment.
UT	V	1–6	5	Voluntary at School Level	In Place	Performance (100)	Stand alone assessment	Carol Ann Goodson (ED) 801-538-7793	Part of Core Curriculum.
WA	D,M,T,V	7–12		TBA	2004		Stand alone assessment	Gina May (ED) 360-753-7389	Part of education reform.

Key

Disciplines
D: Dance
M: Music
T: Theatre
V: Visual Arts
L: Literature

Purposes
1: Graduation requirement/diploma endorsement
2: State profile of student achievement
3: Student accountability
4: School/District accountability
5: Improvement of instruction

Item types
Multiple Choice: Single correct answer from 4–5 possible answers
Selected Response: Includes multiple-choice, matching, true-false, or *Likert Scale*
Performance: Performance activities or tasks
Short Constructed Response: Short written, drawn, danced, acted, or musical answer
Extended Constructed Response: Essay or longer written, drawn, danced, acted, or musical answer

the 324th High School Examination on "Comprehensive Art" (Three Years). Part I (45 minutes) consisted of completing 20 matching items from a list of 25 possible names and terms with another list of 20. Part II was a performance measure that asked the student to pick one question from three options and either complete a painting, a design, or a craft project in the 2 hours and 15 minutes provided.

In the 1970s, the State of Michigan developed a statewide assessment for art and music (grades 4–7–10) that employed individual performance activities that were scored by local arts educators. Led by Ed Roeber, then the head of the Michigan Department of Education's Assessment Program, and based on his experience with the NAEP, the assessment proved that states could conduct and score a large-scale effort and deal with student work in many forms using limited state resources. Like many efforts to make the arts part of the "system," the Michigan assessment never achieved the status of a full assessment for all students due to budget and time concerns.

The NAEP arts assessment was a national assessment. It is unlike most other large-scale assessments in that it creates a national profile of what American students know and can do in a variety of subject areas through assessing a random sample of students from across the country. No one student takes the whole assessment, and students answer or take part in different "blocks" or related sets of exercises. When the student response data are brought together or aggregated, the answers form a mosaic of information. From the mosaic created by the answers of the small sample, inferences can be made about how the entire population might perform if they were all tested.

Preparation for the 1997 NAEP in arts education began in August 1991 when the National Assessment Governing Board (NAGB) (with the encouragement and financial support of the National Endowment for the Arts [NEA] and the Getty Center for Education in the Arts) voted to make arts education the subject of a National Assessment of Educational Progress national assessment.

The framework and specification for the NAEP arts assessment were developed over an eighteen-month period from October 1992 through March 1994. Based on the new National Standards for Arts Education, the assessment was designed for 4th-, 8th-, and 12th-grade students in the areas of dance, music, theatre, and the visual arts using a variety of assessment methods and student response modes. Immediately after the assessment blueprint was completed in March 1994, the preparation of the assessment was begun, and the first round of field tests was conducted in 1995. After a one-year setback due to budget shortfalls, the assessment was conducted in 1997 but only at the eighth-grade level and only given to a national sample of students for art and music and to a selected sample of students in theatre.

The scale-back to eighth grade only was attributed to budget problems, and the elimination of dance was attributed to a paucity of dance programs and a suitable sample at this level.

In 1991 after the NAEP in the arts was announced, the Council of Chief State School Officers invited states to form a group to parallel and take advantage of the NAEP efforts. As the NAEP was being prepared, states interested in arts assessment began an effort to create appropriate arts assessments for state and local levels. The State Collaborative on Assessment and Student Standards (SCASS) Arts consortium was initially formed with 15 states and, in 1994, participated in the development of NAEP assessment exercises. Today, a group of 13 states including New Jersey continues the work.

According to Large-Scale Arts Assessment in the States survey conducted this past summer, thirteen states (but not necessarily all in the SCASS consortium) have, or are developing, assessments. Each has a unique approach that ranges from Oklahoma's 100-item multiple-choice format to Minnesota's plan to give and score their assessment at the local level using performance-based material and rubrics developed at the state level.

Overall, trends for state level assessments in all areas of the curriculum seem to be following one of two distinct paths. Some states are eliminating the more expensive performance measures that create richer achievement information in favor of the less expensive and easier-to-score selected response formats. Others are trying to accommodate more comprehensive or blended efforts that prescribe different roles and different methods for the state, district, and classroom assessments that could represent different pieces of the same mosaic of student achievement.

One thing is for sure: student assessment in some form will be a driving force in the continuing school reform effort. But to use an analogy favored by Elliot Eisner, weighing a cow doesn't make it fatter—and assessment itself will not create better schools. It's the diet that counts for the cow, and it's a combination of factors that need to be addressed for nurturing and improving arts education.

Improvement will come when a critical mass of arts educators participate in a process to:

1. raise the quality of the arts education curriculum, instruction, and assessments.
2. increase the time we allocate to the arts and the training and assistance we provide for arts teachers.
3. attract and retain good arts teachers in the profession.
4. change the public's perceptions of and priorities for arts education.

This is not just a daunting destination but an arduous journey as well.

Frank S. Philip is senior associate at the Council of Chief State School Officers in Washington, D.C. This article originally appeared in the May 2000 issue of New Jersey's Tempo. *Reprinted by permission.*

Grading, Instruction, and Assessment in Music

by Mel Pontious

When attending workshops dealing with newer forms of assessment, many teachers ask the question, "How will this help me grade my students?" Typically these are teachers with fine programs who are super-busy with all the small and large tasks that are part of such a program. They often regard grading as a distraction from the more important job of instruction and are earnestly looking for, and need, a better way of documenting student learning. This column will discuss some of the contradictions inherent in traditional grading and describe a different approach to instruction and assessment that teachers have found enhances student motivation and achievement while avoiding the problems of the typical grading environment.

Grades "R" Us

The concern about grading described above is something like being concerned about the tip of an iceberg, with most of the problem much deeper. The busy ensemble director, intent on preparing students for performance, will naturally develop grading strategies that take a minimum amount of time and constitute a minimum distraction from the task at hand. Examples include attendance and tardy records, practice time outside of rehearsals, points accumulated through various activities, and pencil-and-paper tests. While the first three items are based on worthy assumptions, all are proxies for "doing" music and are not closely linked with the deeper concerns of instruction. They don't deal directly with the musical processes of performing, creating, or responding and often become the focus of student efforts in place of musical processes, skills, and understandings.

The other item above, pencil-and-paper tests, generally focuses on factors that can be represented by easily quantifiable units, assessed by relatively low-level questions, and "graded" by letters or numbers. These *may* be suitable for ascertaining low-level knowledge of basic facts and concepts but hardly useful for determining students' mastery of the complex of procedural and declarative knowledge necessary for performing, creating, or responding. This can best be assessed by having students perform, create, *and* respond.

Grading's "Catch 22"

The most pervasive problem with traditional grades is that the grade, not mastery, becomes the main concern. Even grading students on performance of a segment of music from a piece in progress or giving a weekly lesson/section grade can have unintended results. While both involve "doing" music, which is good, the focus often becomes "getting a grade" for students by having them *prove* their competence. This places the teacher and student in an adversarial position. For the student, this "proving" for a grade tends to be a short-term, but dominant, concern instead of the longer-term mastery of those skills and understandings so necessary for students to *improve* their competency.

Further, research shows that the focus on grades tends to devalue the learning itself. The grade becomes an extrinsic motivator, and when the grade itself is viewed as a reward, creativity, risk-taking, and careful attention to process are lost in favor of speed and the safe response. In fact, the itch for learning, so evident in the early elementary years, gradually disappears in later years when extrinsic rewards like grades get greater emphasis. In addition, grades tend to sort and categorize students into winners and losers, without the redeeming grace of giving students detailed understandings of their strengths and challenges.

A Different Focus

If our job as music educators is to help students become self-sufficient musicians, to make ourselves "dispensable," a change in perspective is needed. The earlier question—"How will this help me grade my students?"—deals only with the tip of the problem. The complete answer involves a deeper matter: restructuring instruction/assessment to deal more directly with ways to *improve* student competence. To realize the benefit of a basic element of the standards movement ("All students can learn …"), a change in focus from "grade-based" education to mastery of the standards is needed. And teachers who have begun teaching in this way find greater student intrinsic motivation *and* achievement.

Because this premise of the standards movement—that all students can learn but in different ways and at different rates—elevates students' individual learning styles and rates in importance, the students themselves must assume a stronger role in directing their own learning. And since mastery for all is the goal, assessment in standards-based education must be linked closely to instruction and be used to inform:

1. students where they are, relative to mastery of the various aspects of the discipline, so *they* may direct their efforts more effectively.
2. teachers, so they may *facilitate* the students' efforts more effectively.
3. parents and other stakeholders, of progress.

Instruction and assessment, then, must be focused on mastery, not grades, with assessment *embedded* in instruction so that assessment itself becomes an episode of instruction and learning.

Instructional Projects

What would "embedded assessment" look like? The following instructional project is an example of an approach that has been quite successful for many teachers. Probably the most important stan-

dards for empowering students to direct their own learning are Standards 6 and 7: *Listening and Analyzing* and *Evaluating*. Students can develop these abilities most readily through assessing their own performing and creating activities, a function that teachers often take over when offering specific tempo and dynamics cues. In the example mentioned, students assessed tapes of their own (or their ensembles') performance *on a regular basis,* with the teacher assessing and providing feedback on the students' critiques as well as their performances. Assessment is thus embedded in an instructional task, with ongoing assessment providing direction for students' further learning and teachers' instructional efforts. And since achievement of any of Standards 1 through 7 will require effort over time, this suggests that it be a long-term project that will parallel and reinforce the usual preparations for performance. It will have a double effect. In the short term it will enhance the next performance, and in the long term the student will develop and refine the abilities to analyze, evaluate, and make good musical judgments (a win-win situation!).

Teachers using this approach note several points:

- Instead of *distracting* from the goal of improving individual or group performance, this instructional/assessment task aligns directly with it.
- Students see this as a meaningful, authentic task, i.e., one that adult professionals do routinely.
- Instead of a teacher-made exercise to "get a grade," with the teacher in an adversarial "prove it" relationship with the students, the students and teacher *collaborate* in achieving the shared goal of a good performance.
- Students exercise a degree of control of their own learning in this project, and research, as well as the experience of Wisconsin teachers, indicates that student autonomy, authentic tasks, and collaborative effort contribute to intrinsic motivation, ownership, and enhanced achievement.

Processfolios

Finally, an excellent learning *and* assessment strategy is a process-portfolio kept by each student. It might contain critiques, tapes of performances, questionnaires, curricular work, journal entries, etc. Portfolio assessment affords a close match between what has been taught and what is assessed. Portfolios also provide a learning opportunity for students—revisiting past work and reflecting on what worked, what didn't, and what would improve it. It can help the student determine a direction for future work as well as form the basis for self- and teacher/student-assessment. And it is an excellent means for informing parents and other stakeholders of student achievement.

About that grading question ...

The answer to the question, "Will this help me grade my students?" is "Yes, but only if the emphasis of instruction and assessment is changed." All of the teachers whose work I have described above have to give letter grades, but they are generally able to focus their students on mastery of musical understandings and processes instead of competition for grades. Several have succeeded in this by using a "learning profile," a teacher/student listing of the goals of the project (e.g., technique, performance skills, music-reading skills, error detection, critiquing, composing, etc.). Both student and teacher assess the portfolio's collection of work on these dimensions and arrive at an agreement on student progress (another excellent learning experience!), which can *then* be translated into a grade. Note that the benefit to learning occurs *before* the grade is established. Such an assessment dwells on what students *have* learned, not what they have failed to learn. And parents are highly supportive of this approach when their children explain their portfolios to them. Displays of student portfolios at concerts, student-generated program notes, student analyses of compositions for the audience—all are excellent ways of communicating to parents and the public-at-large the depth of students' learning.

The instruction and assessment strategies described above are based on combining the Arts PROPEL[1] and CMP[2] models. Teachers in Wisconsin and across the country are discovering the advantages of these approaches, and many teacher educators are including this approach as part of their methods courses. Such an instructional/assessment model provides rich, in-depth learning, and learning profiles such as that described above are more informative and useful to students, teachers, and parents than a single-letter grade.

We live in exciting times! The changes in education that are possible through the standards initiative can lead to situations in which students assume a greater role in their own education, and all students achieve high standards!

Notes

1. ArtsPROPEL is an instruction/assessment model developed by Harvard Project Zero that stresses students' active engagement in their own learning. For more information, contact Project Zero, 671-495-4342.

2. Comprehensive Musicianship through Performance is a model developed in Wisconsin in 1977 for teaching musical understandings in the performance class. For more information, contact WMEA, 608-249-4566.

Mel Pontious is state music consultant for the Department of Public Instruction in Wisconsin. This article originally appeared in the September 1998 issue of Wisconsin School Musician. *Reprinted by permission.*

Is Assessment in Music Appropriate in the Early Childhood Years?

by Frances Rauscher

Assessment in music is often overlooked or avoided in the early childhood years because it appears to be incompatible with a child-centered, process-oriented philosophy that is characteristic of education for young children. A reflective assessment procedure, however, can inform the early childhood teacher's practice of guiding learning in music. Artistic profiles of individual children's accomplishments can center on processes such as discovery, pursuit, perception, communication, self-awareness, social-awareness, skill use, creativity, analysis, and critique. Qualitative, observation-based assessment provides a means with which to provide feedback to children, parents, and educational administrators about individual and group achievements.

In a comprehensive early childhood educational program, children learn to make sense of their worlds through controlled attempts to explore, develop, and express ideas and concepts through performance and action (Alper, 1987; Smith, 1980). In all subject areas, the emphasis is on learning through direct experience and experimentation. The same is true in music, where the learning process revolves around acting-out: using the body and voice to imagine and to represent meaning through the integration of thoughts, sensations, and symbol systems. Often, learning is a private experience, but teachers can assist young children to develop complex musical skills, such as discrimination, through the development of a musical vocabulary and through reflection upon the creative process, aesthetic qualities, evaluation of products, and recognition that there is no one right way to answer a musical problem.

The products or actions of a child, however, can only provide an impression of what the child has learned during a musical experience. Therefore, to review a child's knowledge of music based on the product alone would overlook other important components of musicality and the complex, multileveled skills that are involved in learning. For young children in particular, music must be conceived as a total and integrated experience that warrants the employment of a global form of assessment (McLeod, 1990). Evidence for evaluation and reflection must be gathered over a period of time and focus on numerous musical experiences and works. The manner in which this is achieved is a complex process, one which is made difficult in the early childhood years by the need for the teacher to make sensitive interpretations of children's behavior.

Observation and Interpretation as a Basis for Assessment and Evaluation

In early childhood education, assessment is closely linked to program evaluation. On a daily basis, the teacher plans the curriculum and makes evaluations and programming changes that are based upon young children's learning. In other words, what the child gains from one experience helps the teacher to determine the next learning event. When working with older children, the process of evaluation and program development is made easy by the students' ability to reflect on and discuss their work, often undertaken as long-term projects. The limited verbal skills of young children and the relatively short duration of activities, however, require the teacher to interpret behavior and learning outcomes on the basis of observations that are considered within the context of the cognitive, social, and physical development of young children.

The majority of evaluation and assessment procedures used in early childhood education derive from phenomenological and qualitative-naturalistic traditions (Alexander, 1982; Almy & Genishi, 1979). Participant observation in classrooms requires the same data collection techniques that are used in other settings, including interviewing, observing, documenting, analyzing products, and counting events. These techniques enable the teacher-investigator to understand the meaning of musical experiences through the eyes of the child-participant. This requires the adult to adopt the child's perspective: to think, imagine, perceive, fantasize, create, conceptualize, and use symbols as the child would.

General Artistic Processes That Are Applicable to Music

Nine general artistic processes can be identified which closely resemble the musical interests and abilities of young children. These processes have been implied or described in part by several writers (e.g., Gardner, 1990; McArdle & Barker, 1990) and are outlined below:

1. Discovery
Discovery involves observing, exploring options with a range of materials, comparing, questioning, seeing possibilities, finding alternatives, and seeking purpose.

2. Pursuit
Pursuit involves entering into musical activities, taking initiative, focusing on specific ideas, exploring in depth, staying on task, being goal-directed, problem solving, generating ideas and carrying them out, working hard, and developing a musical idea over time or around personal themes.

3. Perception
Perception involves showing sensory awareness, illustrating sensitivity to physical properties and qualities of materials and the environment, "hearing inside the head," internalizing movement, making fine discriminations, showing care and attention to detail, and evidencing sensitivity to a variety of genres, cultures, and historical periods.

4. Communication
Communication involves selecting and using musical materials and elements with intent, expressing ideas or feeling through the musical medium, and using symbols.

5. Self-Awareness and Social-Awareness
Self-awareness and social-awareness involve working independently, tapping into personal feelings, participating in preparation and clean-up, sharing discoveries, tolerating frustration, participating in group activities, cooperating, communicating effectively, negotiating, empathizing, appreciating other people's contributions, and making suggestions.

6. Skill Use
Skill use involves manipulating materials; showing muscular coordination; controlling basic techniques; showing sensitivity to the elements, principles, and processes of music; showing aesthetic sensitivity; and demonstrating a sense of standards and quality.

7. Creativity
Creativity involves responding to different situations flexibly, seeing afresh, enjoying, taking risks with the musical medium, using imagination, and showing inventiveness.

8. Transfer
Transfer involves describing to others what is seen, heard, felt, thought, or imagined; articulating musical goals; reflecting on process and product; showing interest in hearing and using musical terminology; relating learning to previous learning; contributing personal opinions; and changing direction and attitudes if necessary.

9. Critique
Critique involves appreciating artistic products; talking about one's own artistry and the works of peers; accepting and incorporating suggestions where appropriate; using the processes of describing, interpreting, and judging; and using the work of others for ideas and inspiration.

While a hierarchy within the list is not implied—each aspect being important in itself—there is an implicit order of complexity. Critiquing, for example, requires a higher-level skill than Discovery. Yet, even young children demonstrate the ability to critique (Cole & Schaefer, 1990). The process or processes used in any activity will also depend on the child's developmental level. In addition, each descriptor has meaning only when viewed in the context of the learning environment, teaching practices and methods, and curriculum organization and content. For example, Discovery will be more easily achieved in a learning environment in which children are encouraged to ask questions, explore ideas, and imagine new possibilities than in one in which such processes are not valued.

These nine processes can be used as a basis for assessment, although they are not a prescriptive framework for assessment. They can help teachers to understand musical processes, to recognize how they are used by young children, to focus on processes which will assist children to learn about music, and to explain children's musical development to parents and others.

In addition, the list can be used as a basis for interacting with, or providing feedback to, children about their musical experiences and products. The most valuable feedback that a child can receive is in the form of comments that occur during, or immediately after, a child's musical experience and that involve reflection upon what the child has produced and experienced rather than comments which are information-giving. For example, rather than asking a child to name the notes being played, the teacher might ask open-ended questions and model, label, and extend the child's present understanding. In other words, whether a child is creating a rhythmic pattern on a drum or singing to a CD, comments such as "Good girl!" or "Excellent work!" may be encouraging, but they are not descriptive or explanatory, nor do they enhance a child's awareness of musical processes, elements, concepts, or forms of expression.

A Final Comment

When used as the basis for assessment, observations made of each of the nine processes provide qualitative data about the child that enables a teacher to judge the effectiveness of the musical program being offered. Teachers and other early childhood staff are accustomed to observing and recording children's behavior to inform curriculum development, implementation, and evaluation and typically select materials and learning experiences to accommodate each child's level of development and interest. However, observations of musical programs are typically undertaken less than in other curriculum areas, but they are equally important to understanding how children apply the musical processes to create personal meaning,

to generating feedback to the children, and to providing a basis for planning learning experiences. Observations must be specific and must focus on:

a. the child's learning experience described through anecdotal information
b. artistic elements that the child might use during the process
c. the nine processes described above
d. planning implications.

To synthesize the data, an observation sheet may be developed to reflect the grammar, syntax, sensory systems, and media of music's unique expression.

To participate in arts education with this level of understanding, it is not sufficient for teachers of young children to be advocates for music; they must also have a deep knowledge of music and practice the processes of musicality. Unless the importance of literacy in music in early childhood is recognized, children may progress through school without having significant learning experiences. Furthermore, many children who may have the natural proclivity to excel in music may not have a chance to recognize their potential if they do not receive adequate exposure to music and inspiration from educators who are responsive participants.

References

Alexander, R. R. (1982). Participant observation, ethnography, and their use in educational evaluation: A review of selected works. *Studies in Art Education, 24,* 63–69.

Almy, M., & Genishi, C. (1979). *Ways of studying children* (Rev. ed.). New York: Teachers College Press.

Alper, C. C. (1987). Early childhood music education. In C. Seefeldt (Ed.), *The early childhood curriculum: A review of current research* (pp. 237–50). New York: Teachers College Press.

Cole, E. S., & Schaefer, C. (1990). Can young children be art critics? *Young children, 45,* 33–38.

Gardner, H. (1990, Dec.). *Assessment of student learning in the arts.* Paper presented at the Evaluation and Assessing the Visual Arts in Education Conference, Bosschenhoofdt, Netherlands.

McArdle, F., & Barker, B. (1990). *What'll I do for art today?* Melbourne: Nelson.

McLeod, J. (1990). *The arts and the year 2000*. Brisbane: Queensland Department of Education.

Smith, N. (1980). Classroom practice: Creating meaning in the arts. In J. J. Hausman (Ed.), *Arts and the schools* (pp. 79–116). New York: McGraw-Hill.

Frances Rauscher is assistant professor of psychology at the University of Wisconsin–Oshkosh. This article originally appeared in the September 1998 issue of Wisconsin School Musician. *Reprinted by permission.*

Assessment FAQs for Music Educators

by Carlos Xavier Rodriguez

One of the greatest frustrations about assessment is determining the appropriate level at which to describe it. On the one hand, we want assessment to be fully integrated into the learning process, which suggests that it must take many forms, serve many needs, involve lots of people, and be ongoing. On the other hand, improving upon traditional assessment models and exchanging ideas among educators require some precise thinking about the specific role of assessment in music instruction. These opposing forces often curtail meaningful progress in assessment design and implementation. Indeed, discussing assessment creates as many new questions as it answers. To help alleviate this problem, I have created a list of FAQs ("Frequently Asked Questions") for assessment in music education. It is offered with the hope that it will bring some clarity to this often ambiguous topic and also stimulate discussion about some of the new ideas that now dominate this area of instruction.

What is assessment?

The MENC publication of assessment strategies for the National Standards defines assessment as "the overall process of making analytical judgments [that] ... emphasizes discernment and discrimination: it is best carried out using a variety of techniques."[1] In the September 1999 *Music Educators Journal* (a Special Focus issue on this topic), Edward Asmus defines assessment as "the collection, analysis, interpretation, and application of information about student performance or program effectiveness in order to make educational decisions."[2] These two definitions imply that assessment is the way in which we discover how much our students have learned, how well they have learned it, and to what extent this progress is attributable to the materials, the instruction, and the learning environment.

So then, what's the difference between assessment and evaluation?

Evaluation is a part of assessment—that part in which you make a judgment about the evidence you have collected through assessment. However, quite often assessment and evaluation are used interchangeably to refer to essentially the same activity, which, although convenient, carries the disadvantage of misleading people into thinking that assessment is merely the act of "giving a grade" to something. One reason why the term "assessment" causes uneasiness is that it should serve a basic function in instruction, yet every time we turn around it seems to imply more than it did before.

What gets assessed?

If we set aside curriculum, teaching, and large-scale classroom-level assessment for the moment and speak in terms of individual students, the traditional areas for assessment in music have been knowledge, skills, and responses, which correspond to cognitive, manipulative, and affective domains of learning. Since we are in a "performance-based" educational phase, the term "standards" has been adopted for the indicators we use to determine student growth. More recent assessment literature often uses the terms "content" and "performance" standards to delineate the knowledge and skills, respectively, needed in any subject area. However, we must remember that some competencies in music do not fall neatly into one or the other category, such as the extent to which students are able to formulate and articulate musical preferences. This reminds us that even the most recent assessment models still require additional refinement before they accommodate the complexity of musical thinking.

What are some of the "new ideas" in assessment that I should know about?

Most educators agree that assessment should be "authentic," which means that it invokes the problems, tools, and conditions that students are likely to encounter in the "real world." Assessment experts have observed that students recognize authentic tasks when they see them and are thus more inclined to do their best work.

Some educators believe that the larger the assessment time frame, the more revealing the information will be regarding higher-order thinking skills. For this reason, extended projects and portfolios are in high favor, although the time investment for monitoring these documents is staggering. Further, the types of musical activities for which extended projects are appropriate are not always clear. For instance, the development of a musical composition is highly suitable, but learning scale fingerings, while possible, is not nearly as compelling. Generally, the more the activity requires creative thinking skills, the more suitable it is for long-term assessment techniques.

One of the hallmarks of progressive assessment is the use of "constructed response" items that require students to create, rather than select, solutions to musical problems. This assessment feature is problematic for educators who do not endorse the concept of multiple correct answers or are not fond of creative tasks in general. The rationale is that students are more likely to invoke "everything they know" about music if they must invent and execute a solution to a musical problem.

The extraordinary cultural diversity of American society has forced us to be mindful of "fairness" in assessment. An assessment strategy is fair if it does not give advantage to factors that are irrelevant to the learning process and environment. Fairness thus increases the reliability of assessments. Conversely, there is also a movement to provide alternative assessment strategies that are relevant to students' ethnic background, gender, age, and special needs. These two concerns are equally served by music educators who provide consistently flexible options for assessments, such as allowing all children to select their own song materials or tools for demonstrating specific performing or describing skills, or eliminating time constraints on certain assessment tasks.

What should I consider when formulating new assessment procedures?

Brevity

The simpler and more straightforward, the better. The less time taken for explanation of a problem, the more time students have to work on their solutions. Simplified explanations also reveal the time taken to make them that way, which likewise encourages students to exercise greater care in their responses. The language you use to present your assessment technique has a significant effect on the quality of student performance and resulting information.

Credibility

Enlisting the help of students, teachers, administrators, and parents—the recipients of assessment results—will boost the acceptance of your new assessment technique. Emphasizing why and how your ideas represent an improvement over existing practices helps others understand better why your new technique is worthwhile.

Connectivity

The more your assessment strategy is designed to indicate parallel success in other musical and non-musical areas, the more useful that assessment will be in your total school setting. Whether music educators agree with this perspective, the educational community tends to value musicality in terms of its association with other competencies—and this is true of other subjects as well (e.g., reading success is often appreciated as a catalyst for across-the-board success in school).

Finally, what about this idea of "assessment as instruction"?

Perhaps the most crucial of all recommendations for building new assessments in music is the idea that the specific assessment activities *be practiced* in the classroom prior to the assessment.[3] In this way, students are reasonably comfortable with the process, are less distracted, and are poised to do their best work. More importantly, music instruction is enhanced by this arrangement because students are more consistently engaged in constructing, refining, and communicating musical ideas, much like we expect the best musicians to do.

I encourage all music educators to revisit their current assessment strategies and search for ways to make them more effective, more authentic, and more integral to the learning process. There is much to be gained from taking a closer look at what makes our students as musical as they become under our leadership.

Notes

1. Music Educators National Conference, *Performance Standards for Music: Strategies and Benchmarks for Assessing Progress toward the National Standards, Grades PreK–12.* (Reston, VA: MENC, 1996), 1.

2. Edward P. Asmus, "Music assessment concepts," *Music Educators Journal* 86, no. 2 (1999): 19.

3. This point is stressed several times in MENC's *Performance Standards for Music.*

Carlos Xavier Rodriguez is assistant professor of music education at the University of Iowa in Iowa City. This article originally appeared in the September 1999 issue of Iowa Music Educator. *Reprinted by permission.*

Students Can ... Assess

by Leyla Sanyer

Pencil-and-paper tests, practice charts, playing exams and attitude observations: these are systems that music teachers have commonly used to evaluate their students' progress. Many of us have never been very comfortable with these somewhat cumbersome and arbitrary methods. In the Wisconsin CMP (Comprehensive Musicianship through Performance) Project we are always looking for better ways to assess what our students know and the effectiveness of instruction.

It's helpful if we first separate the issue of evaluation from the assessment process. *Evaluation* (sometimes referred to as grading) is the process of analyzing and interpreting data to make judgments about the data. *Assessment* is simply the gathering of data, both quantitative and qualitative. Qualitative data cannot be easily measured but can be documented through the use of portfolios, teacher observation, and performance.

Music teachers constantly make informal assessments in the classroom. We ask questions, listen to individual playing, discuss, and analyze. But many of us haven't considered this to be as important as the grading process. If we focus more on the assessment process, the task of evaluation becomes easier and less subjective!

For a long time the CMP Project has stressed that teachers need to share the instructional planning process with our students. Many of us find that by asking our classes to set their own goals and assess their own progress more substantial learning takes place in the classroom. **Students can:**

- design their own projects and assess them
- write about their goals each week
- listen to tapes of their own playing and critique their own performances

- discuss their progress with the teacher and/or peers
- grade themselves.

Many teachers have discovered the amazing power of peer tutoring within the classroom. We all know that the quickest way to learn something is to go through the process of teaching it. The use of peer assessment is an important component to consider when following the CMP Model. **Students can:**

- listen to concert tapes and write/discuss recommendations for improvement
- break into groups and run their own sectionals
- conduct warm-ups and rehearsals
- learn how to follow positive comments with constructive suggestions
- participate in chamber music rehearsals.

Portfolios have become a popular and useful tool to help students organize their thinking and collect data that demonstrate their knowledge. These collections can take many forms, all of which are useful as an assessment tool for the student and the teacher. **Students can:**

- keep individual performance tapes and critiques
- keep a written log of goals, reflections, and observations
- collect tests, quizzes, and written assignments
- keep a record of projects, both group and individual
- keep a record of concerts attended, performed and critiqued.

Teachers need to look at alternatives to point systems, attitude grading and attendance/practice records. Musical knowledge is as important as performance skills, and student involvement in the process is critical. There are many classroom strategies which can serve as creative and efficient assessments. You can begin to assess student knowledge by using your own questioning skills. **You can:**

- create questions beforehand
- ask questions which require more than a "yes" or "no" answer
- ask questions in sequence so that students can build on their experience
- ask a question and then allow "wait" time before calling on a specific student
- try to direct questions at every student, not just the ones who love to answer
- ask open-ended questions that may have multiple answers
- avoid evaluative responses to students' answers.

There are other fun classroom strategies that can serve as assessments. Sometimes just asking students to reflect on something helps them to assess themselves. **You can also:**

- ask the class to take out a piece of music by describing some characteristic of the piece other than the title or composer
- sight-read or rehearse a similar piece and check for the transfer of concepts

- pose a problem and ask students to write down their ideas on 3 x 5 cards.

Some assessments occur *before* the study of a piece. These involve goal setting and questioning. Other assessments occur during the rehearsal process. Reflection, discussion and more goal setting are common here. The assessments that occur after the learning process are those with which we are perhaps most familiar. These include exams, critiques, completed projects, observations and assignments.

There is one more long-term assessment we should not forget, however. *How are our students developing as independent musicians, and do they continue to use music throughout their lives?* Try holding a 10-year reunion and inviting all alumni to bring their own or borrowed instruments. Run a rehearsal in the afternoon, serve a potluck dinner and present a short concert. We did it at our high school this spring. Over two-thirds of those invited were able to attend, and it was very exciting to see how pivotal musical experiences still are in their lives. Talk about a strong assessment!

Leyla Sanyer is orchestra director at Oregon High School in Oregon, Wisconsin. This article originally appeared in the September 1998 issue of Wisconsin School Musician. *Reprinted by permission.*

Accountability and Assessment in the Music Classroom

by Christine Sezer

The increased demands by the general public for better results from our educational system and more educational value for our tax dollars have effected the issues of accountability. Just exactly what is accountability? Should teachers really be held responsible for the success or failure of their students? What are your thoughts?

With the onset of the New Jersey Core Curriculum Content Standards in performing and visual arts now in place, assessment of these standards is a main goal of the New Jersey Department of Education. Students in grades four, eight and eleven are being assessed (1999, 2000, 2001 and 2002), beginning with a field test in the fall of 1999.

In some respects, music teachers have always been accountable for their students' accomplishments and successes. But in other respects, accountability may be an entirely new issue to be faced regarding the upcoming statewide assessment tests. Accountability impacts curriculum planning, instructional strategies, budgets, behavioral objectives, individualized learning and program evaluation as well as student evaluation.

Current problems in our educational system include: many students have not completed school (dropping out before graduating); many have not developed occupational skills which will enable them to earn a living and make a positive contribution to our society; many have not developed basic skills in reading, writing and math; many have not developed verbal and written communication skills that are essential to performing well in any job market. Thus, the demand for accountability has grown. Yet, in all these demands, the expectation of accountability in the arts in the past has not been a major concern. Music programs were a responsibility of school districts, but since they were not usually identified as problem areas, accountability was not a major priority. This trend is definitely not the case any more—published results of assessment tests in music will now be a priority.

Music educators must prepare for the assessment program. We must be able to define the outcomes of our programs and prove that the majority of all our students are meeting the outcomes. We now have excellent statements of the philosophy for which we stand; MENC (Goals 2000) has developed and provided organizational goals and objectives that incorporate and reflect the main concepts, knowledge and skills that should be implemented in our music curriculums. Vague philosophies and goals in local curriculum guides can no longer be accepted as adequate descriptions of an exemplary and accountable music program. In accountability, emphasis is usually placed on student learning outcomes, not so much on teacher performance, teaching strategies and methods, or administrative practices. In other words, what is really judged is output, not input. This is very different from the usual accrediting procedures used in evaluating school systems. Accrediting agencies use input measurements such as teacher-pupil ratio, number of teachers with certificates and master's or doctoral degrees, per-pupil expenditures, types of courses offered, equipment, facilities and administration.

Now the focus is the end product and the proof of performance. Measurement in broad, general terms is no longer acceptable. Clear and precise statements of objectives that are not open to varied interpretations and "second guesses" are a must regarding accountability.

Accountability is a legal, ethical and moral obligation in every profession. In education, a teacher should not be held accountable unless he knows *what he is responsible for*—knowledge and skill statements in curriculum guides must be clearly specified and stated. The outcomes should be agreed upon—teachers should be involved in the development goals and objectives in curriculum guides. Teachers should be committed to the goals and objectives that they set forth; most teachers will not teach toward goals and objectives to which they are not committed. In addition, teachers should have some decision-making power over the resources and materials needed to accomplish their goals and objectives. Teacher input regarding scheduling, facilities, equipment, materials and budget would have an effect on the desired outcomes.

A systematic approach to instruction is desired in order to be realistic when focusing on accountability. Systems of one type or another have been used for years in music education. For example, elementary vocal and instrumental programs at some point or another fill the needs of the middle school and high school performing organizations—"feeder systems" are certainly a systematic planned approach designed to achieve the goal of a successful program as students progress to a higher level of musicianship. These systems are usually group-oriented and emphasize, for the most part, group results rather than individual learning. This is not acceptable for accountability. "The systems approach used for accountability is based on common sense and the nature of man's functioning intellect. Perceptual input through the senses is stored and processed in the brain. On the basis of this information, decisions are made to reach a goal."[1] Then the actual attempt is made to reach the goal. Subsequent action is based upon the success or failure of the attempt.

Don't you agree that common sense helps us to improve ourselves? We certainly can improve ourselves as music teachers when we try new methods, materials, teaching strategies and techniques to achieve our teaching goals and evaluate their effectiveness. We get an idea (original or from a colleague, workshop, book, journal or conference); we try it; we see how it works; if it is

successful, we keep it and modify it; if it is not successful, we don't use it again. Not a very intricate or detailed process, but it is using our *common sense.*

The following components are part of accountability: (1) behavioral objectives that state *what each student should know and be able to do* at the end of instruction, (2) preassessment (field test) to ascertain *what the student needs to learn,* (3) instructional strategies to facilitate *learning what is not known,* and (4) a post-test (the assessment test) to assess student progress and teaching effectiveness.

The process of accountability is a problem-solving technique that can be applied to any program of curriculum development. "*First,* behavioral objectives are developed—these should be derived from the philosophy and higher-level goals of music education. Write down in general terms the broad aims and purposes of the course and validate them against higher-level educational goals (knowledge and skill statements based on set standards). These objectives need not change the course content substantially. However, objectives should indicate specifically *what* students are to do with that content. Objectives should communicate instructional intent, providing guidance for learners and direction for teaching. They help individualize instruction by focusing upon each student. They provide the basis for selecting teaching strategies and for deriving assessment questions. *Second,* specific test items are developed (the field test)—these items will be evidence that learning has occurred. Items are derived directly from the stated objectives."[2] This method of construction should result in high content validity. *Third,* appropriate activities, materials and media are chosen to achieve the objectives. In what tasks should students be involved? With what media (if any) should students interact to provide or support learning experiences? A well-written objective should suggest many alternative learning tasks and instructional media from which final selections can be made. Scheduling of needed time in appropriate time blocks is to be considered. *Fourth,* the field test is administered. This test (preassessment) should indicate what the students have mastered and what they need to refine and learn before the actual assessment test. *Fifth,* selected teaching strategies and instructional media can be explored at this point. Learning effectiveness and student reaction can be observed, and adjustments can be made before the final assessment test. *Sixth,* the assessment test is administered. *Seventh,* analyze and interpret the test data. Individual gain scores are most important for accountability. Has each student attained the objectives?

If the test is valid and students have achieved the objectives, the assessment was successful and accountability was achieved. If this was not the case, you must analyze the reasons for instructional failure. Some possible problems may include: students did not understand the objectives (perhaps the statements were not clear or were ambiguous)—revise statements if needed; instructional strategies were ineffective or inappropriate—provide demonstrations, model expected behavior, enough practice time, appropriate drill material and/or self-evaluation; media was not effective or used properly—get assistance from a media specialist; test items were not valid—rework the test items to reflect the instruction.

As a member of the New Jersey State Assessment Committee, I have learned and experienced a great deal regarding the process of assessment and accountability. At previous workshop presentations I have encountered many teachers who have little or no experience in assessment or accountability. Some resent the idea that their successful music programs and proven teaching methods should be assessed. Some feel threatened and insecure. This results in a negative attitude toward the assessment project. Some feel apathetic and that too much is being required in a very short time in terms of preparation for the assessment test. The test is really a *good* and *valuable* effort to raise the standards and expectations of the arts in our state. Good teachers have been accountable forever—they have always worked hard using materials and appropriate methods to help their students achieve curriculum goals successfully. Music teachers as a group have always been held more accountable than other teachers in the school—their musical organizations must perform in public and be evaluated many times each year. Concerts, half-time shows, programs, and festival and competition ratings provide ample proof of results of group accountability. However, group performance alone is no longer accepted as a measure of musical accountability.

Accountability means that music teachers are responsible for the learning of each pupil as an individual, as well as for the training of bands, orchestras and choruses. Accountability is not a negative concept.

A positive application opens up many possibilities at all levels of the music program. With its related systems approach to education, accountability should help good teachers do an even better job. Accountability and assessment present a challenge and a certain excitement to your existing program. It can mean the following positive outcomes to you and your teaching: (1) You are in control of the teaching/learning situation. (2) You develop learning and performance objectives for student learning. (3) You develop procedures; you try to revise them on the basis of assessment results. (4) You *cause* learning to occur; you have evidence of results. (5) You no longer go through a method book lesson by lesson—you create more of your own strategies, methods and techniques. (6) Your students move at their own pace—exceptionally talented students are not held back by others. (7) You do not have to teach the "way you were taught"—you teach for the objectives to which you are committed. (8) You can change the way you see your students—the approach is positive and optimistic because you are *causing* and *inspiring* your students to learn. (9) You are concerned with each child. Mastery of learning requires *individual achievement*. Excellence in music teaching has always been concerned with musical objectives, effective methods, materials and evaluation—thus, *accountability*—you commit to improve your teaching and student learning. You decide *what* students should be able to *know* and do after instruction. You teach them. Then, *you prove that they know, understand and can do what you have taught them!*

Teaching music—it's worth it!

References

1. Lessinger, Leon, and Tyler, Ralph. (1991). *Accountability in education.* Worthington, OH: Jones Publishing Company.

2. Lobuta, Joseph. (1989). *The accountability umbrella.* Detroit, MI: Wayne State University Press.

Christine Sezer is general music teacher and choral director at Howell Township Middle School North in Farmingdale, New Jersey. This article originally appeared in the March 1999 issue of New Jersey's Tempo. *Reprinted by permission.*

Assessment Tool for Individuals in Performing Ensembles

by Craig P. Sherman

Do you cringe when you hear the phrase "assessment" or "portfolio?" Do you hope that upon waking one day these terms will have disappeared from the educational vocabulary? I did, too, until one day I realized that these terms will not go away and on some level we have to deal with the refinement of this evaluative process. To this end, I devised a tool that works for me; it may work for you also. Any process can be valid if it works for one's individual and unique situation. Given the vast number of subtle variations in scheduling, awarding of credit, and procedural formats, it is improbable to believe that there is a singular tool that is universal.

Before a discussion on assessment can occur, there are a few items that need to be clarified. Many states have laws that do not allow for attendance to be a criteria for assessment, evaluation, and eventual grading. These attendance laws have been challenged and subsequently upheld by the courts. As ridiculous as this ruling may appear to the professional educator, it is indeed statutory. Therefore, we [educators] have found a variety of means to accommodate the attendance issue; the most functional of which may be classroom participation.

Another issue ensemble conductors have to deal with is the fact that we associate with our students in a realm of their being so vastly different from any other teacher with whom they work. This additional affective relationship is often one of the reasons we enter the field of music education, yet at the same time it thrusts us into a subjective area in terms of assessment and grading.

This gray area can be one of the most frustrating and anxiety-producing parts of our positions as music teachers. How do I effectively and fairly grade in an area that is arguably primarily subjective and opinion-driven? We can all agree that good intonation, clean technique, and solid preparation are not subjective. However, beyond the relatively few concrete aspects of aesthetic music education, much of what we do and how we assess is based on our professional opinion. In today's litigious society, that may not be enough.

A very critical concern for all of us is time. How much of my rehearsal will be consumed while I attend to the process of student assessment? How many additional hours will be required to complete this task? None! The great part about this system is that it requires no rehearsal time or real effort beyond what is current practice. Whatever system we use to keep records of tardiness or other necessary school-related tasks can also be used for assessment. What works for me (immediately after the rehearsal, when necessary) is making notations in my grade book that correspond to those categories on my assessment form (see the sidebar). I simply use a representative plus or minus next to the student's name as his or her performance warrants, as that system is easy, quick, and recognizable. And, even then, the notation is only necessary if the individual's classroom conduct falls at either end of the positive or negative continuum. Any deportment in between is not noteworthy, as it is either normal expectation or handled in the natural course of our rehearsal. Rarely is an explanatory note necessary, but one may need to be included on occasion. The only additional work required for this system to function well is at the time of grading. We must perform that duty anyway, so we have already accommodated for it.

Performing ensembles function in much the same manner as sport teams. The extraneous benefits of the multitude of group skills in both these genres of experiences are well-touted and documented. Indirectly then, ensemble directors are also coaches. The clear difference, however, is that coaches are usually extra-curricular, while music directors are curricular; we must grade. The athletic analogy, however, is more clear and valid if directors are analogized to physical educators. We are comparable in that we must assess. This appraisal is based on a balance of natural ability and talent, as well as individual work ethic and effort, yet the two do not necessarily correlate.

This valuation is not an easy task, as we have encountered students who tip the scale to one side or the other. The difficulty lies in grading a student on either side of the balance fairly. Accordingly, in an informal and unscientific phone sample, an astounding 90 percent of high schools surveyed grade their physical education students on a pass–fail method. This system of grading eliminates most of the concerns over which music ensemble directors must agonize at the end of each quarter and semester.

What can we do? How do we evaluate and grade in an equitable way so that we can account for these variables and can also help keep ourselves out of the court system? The first phase is to devise a personal form to suit the individual situation and also to prioritize specific criteria (see sidebar for example of assessment rubric). While this process sounds like a Brobdingnagian task, once one identifies and prioritizes the most significant daily tasks and performance indicators, it actually makes assessment more objective and manageable.

The importance of a rubric is that it makes the subjective aspects of the assessment process more concrete. While portions of how one determines the scoring within the rubric may be opinion and somewhat subjective, the overall process and results become more clearly understood in this manner. It is imperative to discuss the form, criteria, and rubrics with the students early in the year or semester. Additionally, the performance indicators must be explained and conveyed to all involved in the process to establish clarity, understanding, and acceptance. This disclosure eliminates any bewilderment at grading time.

The criteria upon which the students' assessment and consequent grades are based need to be established with the serious consideration of the uniqueness of one's program. The categories within each rubric can be adjusted to better match specific concerns you may have within your own circumstance. There is an overt indication of priorities with regard to your requirements and expectations. The forms merely assess the degree to which the student successfully completes each task. The following forms are rather self-explanatory by design. This clarity gives credibility and validity to the procedure. Students, parents, administrators, and boards of education are more likely to adopt a system that is easily understood. In this process, each student begins with a score of one hundred, hence an A or A-plus, if that is part of your system. This is significant, as it makes no preconceived notion or assumption about a student's ability or prior achievement, performance, or assessments.

Another benefit is that the rubric identifies the skills we teach and reinforce daily to promote higher-order and critical-thinking skills. For example, class participation might include the student devising a warm-up pattern for the day. Another may be determining a solution to a musical difficulty experienced by their section or the group, or it may include any number of activities that we regularly facilitate within our normal rehearsal.

In the definitions of the indicators, there are three items designed specifically for individual assessment, two that are group-specific, and one that is inclusive of both responsibilities. With familiarity, the rubric becomes a tool that encourages student growth, development, and responsibility to self and peers.

This process is begun with the given maximum points in each category. The numerical deduction is taken relative to the student NOT performing to the desired expectation. In this case, you would refer to the notations from the grade book, if there were any. If the student achieved the expected level of the criteria as defined within the rubric, there is no reduction in that category. The process continues for each criteria.

While initially it seems like a great deal of work, in reality it is easier than the arbitrary assigning of grades that may result in the possible risk of being challenged to explain them without any justifying credentials. These documents readily and adequately fulfill that role.

Sample Assessment Rubrics and Form

Assessment Rubrics

The deductions for each category are recorded for each student on the form in column 2.

Rehearsal Technique (15 points): The basic elements of how one reacts, responds, and conducts oneself during rehearsals; also included, how one attends to individual responsibilities to the group.

Class Participation (10 points): Daily involvement in the rehearsal musically, attentively, and responsively.

Preparation/Progress (15 points): The demonstration of consistent improvement and growth as a result of individual work outside the rehearsal.

Performance Demonstrations (10 points): One's performance when asked during the course of a rehearsal either individually or within one's section.

Written Demonstrations (5 points): Any written tests or quizzes, possibly on musical vocabulary, notation, or counting of rhythm patterns.

Performances (25 points): As a performing ensemble, barring extreme emergencies, attendance is mandatory at all performances.

Assessment Form

Name		
Category		**Deduction**
Rehearsal Technique	(15)	_____
Class Participation	(10)	_____
Preparation/Progress	(15)	_____
Performance Demonstrations	(10)	_____
Written Demonstrations	(5)	_____
Performances	(25)	_____

_____
Total Deductions

_____
Grade

By subtracting the total deductions from one hundred, this table, or one that more accurately applies to your individual situation, is used to translate the numerical score to the letter grade.

97–100 = A+	87–89 = B+	77–79 = C+
94–96 = A	84–86 = B	74–76 = C
90–93 = A-	80–83 = B-	70–73 = C-

The blank forms can be copied or saved on computer. If the form is produced as a word-processing document and a database of the members is also maintained, through the use of the mail-merge function on most software suites, it is relatively simple to print out an original form for each student.

While I do not profess that this is the only, or even a better, system of assessing student achievement in a performance-based ensemble than you presently use, it is another viable option. If portfolio assessment is not a terrifying phrase to you and you use that manner of evaluation, then this may serve as another entry within that package. My suggestion is to try it for one quarter or semester prior to total implementation. You may want to attempt a pilot program with only a few students or one ensemble as a control group for yourself to see how well it works before full-scale use. Any procedure like this is impossible to perform or utilize if not presented and clarified early in the semester, year, or relationship. Only then will it serve to strengthen our personal and professional credibility and viability to all with whom we work. Good Luck.

Craig P. Sherman is the director of bands at Scarsdale High School and is pursuing a doctorate at Teachers College, Columbia University, in New York City. This article originally appeared in the October 1999 issue of New York's The School Music News. Reprinted by permission.

Student Self-Assessment in the Middle School Ensemble

by Barbara Simmons

Student self-assessment in the middle school band and orchestra can be an important educational tool. By engaging in self-assessment, students develop important listening skills, as well as learn how to gain ownership for their own learning. Students need both these skills when practicing at home or during a rehearsal.

In order to give the students the tools to self-assess, I have tried to develop a task to monitor student progress in this area. This process has been an ongoing project that I have been developing over the past three years.

The process of student self-assessment begins when students enter class in the 7th grade. The teacher begins by continually asking general questions about the student's performance.

"Could you hear the melody line in the trumpet section?"

"Is the percussion section overpowering the band during this section?"

These are examples of effective teaching strategies used by many teachers during an ensemble rehearsal. Students are immersed in the thought process needed for the self-evaluation of their own playing, as well as how their playing fits in with others' playing.

After continually being asked these types of questions orally during rehearsals, students are asked to do a written critique of their Winter Concert. This process should take about three rehearsals. Most teachers spend time after their concerts playing a video- or audio-recording of the program for the students. This is an excellent time for students to work on a written critique. Students view their portion of the concert a num-

ber of times. The first time students gain a broad overview of their performance. During this viewing they focus on the visual and aural aspects of the performance, while the teacher makes simple comments about their performance.

"Listen to that trumpet line come through; percussion, you did a great job playing pianissimo during that section."

"Clarinets, the intonation on that one passage in the trio that we worked on was perfect; every one of you played in tune."

At the end of this viewing session, the teacher discusses the critical dimensions that students should pay attention to during the next viewing of the tape. These critical dimensions are dynamics, key signature, intonation, articulation, tempo, posture, and balance.

The next rehearsal begins by the class listing the critical dimensions. The teacher then explains what each of these dimensions means. Next it's note-taking time. The students view the tape many times, taking notes on each of the above dimensions. While taking notes, the teacher interjects hints about what they should be looking at or listening for in the music: "We're not together! Listen to hear if you can tell which section rushed the tempo."

One week after the day of the last viewing, the students turn in a written critique. They are graded on their use of music terminology, their detailed use of the indicated critical dimensions, their identification of the strengths and weaknesses of their performance, and their suggestions for how the performance might be improved. This same process is followed after the spring concert. However, students must do their critique with less assistance from the teacher.

In 8th grade, the viewing of the tape from the winter concert is again shown in three rehearsals after the critical dimensions are reviewed. The only difference in the process is that the teacher does not give suggestions during the note-taking. The same grading procedures are used, with greater detail in student responses expected.

By the final spring concert critique, 8th-grade students are asked to write a critique after viewing the concert twice, with no involvement by the teacher. The same grading procedure indicated above is used.

The following are examples of student work using three formats: Narrative, Bulleted Comments, and Grid.

Narrative
Student Critique of *Sunliner*

8th-Grade Band *Sunliner* needed improvement in six of seven elements (dynamics, pitch, articulation, tempo, posture, and balance). The only passable element in my opinion was key signature or correct notes. Throughout the whole song, our dynamics seemed very flat. We needed to bring out the louder notes, but more importantly, hold back in softer parts of the song. One of the best aspects of *Sunliner* was key signature. Just about all of our notes were played correctly. Articulation was another element which needed improvement. The whole song was slurred. Adding more accents and making notes shorter would have improved the sound significantly. The first two notes of the song exemplify this. The first note could have been more crisp, and the second note should have had more of an accent. Our pitch was decent except for the middle section of the song. During the clarinet solo, the trombones were sharp, and the saxophones were flat. In the beginning, we had a steady tempo, and we followed the conductor like clockwork. Flutes came in slightly late on the first note. In the middle, along with being sharp, the trombones were too slow and didn't stay with the clarinets. Possibly, if the trombones had felt a bit more comfortable with their notes and where their slides were supposed to be, they could have kept up with the clarinets. Most of the band didn't have acceptable posture, either. The trombone horns were pointed at the floor, flutes had their backs against the chair, were slouched, and didn't hold their flutes up. Our balance was nice in the beginning. Nobody stood out by being too loud. In the middle, flutes could have been louder, and the rest of the band softer. *Sunliner,* while okay, could have been improved a lot.

Bulleted Comments
Student Critique of *Triptych,* 8th-Grade Orchestra

Dynamics: This should have been more toward *mp* than *mf.* There was one noticeable decrescendo in the middle, but when we crescendoed, it wasn't *f* enough.

Key signature: Very much in tune. This shows that the orchestra has a good feel for the scale of G Major.

Intonation: Very good. The transitions to sharps or flats were very smooth.

Articulation: The piece was very lyrical and legato. Most of the second violin and first violin section had their bowings correct.

Tempo: The piano was wonderful. He was very steady and kept the orchestra together. The song had a nice moderato.

Posture: This was the best of all the four songs.

Balance: Not many people looked up at the conductor. The bass and cellos were too loud during the first violins' melody at the end. The balance before that was wonderful.

Grid
Student Critique of *Amencan Salute,* 7th-Grade Band

Dynamics	• Crescendos at beginning good by trumpets • Trumpets—too forte
Key Signature	• French Horns—a few wrong notes at Intro • Trumpets—two people off at solo
Intonation	• Nice by most; French Horns— way off at solo, two Trumpets— flat, Trombones—flat in Intro
Articulation	• Low Brass solo—too jagged; rest of song good by all
Tempo	• Trumpets—too allegro at solo • Baritone Horn—rushes at Low Brass solo
Posture	• Saxophones—slouched, especially Bari • Trumpets—pointing down
Balance	• Drums—too forte at Intro • Can't hear Low Brass • Good at end

Of the three types of responses, the Narrative takes the most time and is the most difficult to correct. Students with strong linguistic skills have an advantage in this type of response. Engaging students in this approach might be the basis for an effective interdisciplinary project.

On the other hand, the Grid is probably the easiest to grade, taking the least amount of time. The Bulleted Response falls somewhere in between the other two types of responses. It provides students more space for explanation and detail than the Grid but not as much freedom as in the Narrative.

In conclusion, the time spent on this process is well worth the effort. In the long run, it saves time. The student now is able to take the responsibility for his or her own playing, individually as well as in the ensemble. The teacher's role is to give the student the skills to self-assess.

Barbara Simmons teaches middle school instrumental music at Henry James, Jr. Middle School in Simsbury, Connecticut. This article originally appeared in the Spring 1998 issue of Connecticut's CMEA News. *Reprinted by permission.*

Want the Right Answers? Ask the Right Questions!

by Victoria Smith

Assessment in high school general music is not much different from assessment at other levels of general music: we need to know what our students are learning and how effectively they are learning it. An important responsibility, therefore, is designing tools to accurately and effectively make these assessments.

Many of the traditional testing formats that our teachers used to measure learning when we were in school are not very effective instruments for measuring the goals we have for our students. For example, true-or-false, multiple-choice, and fill-in-the-blank questions provide efficient ways to measure the extent to which students have memorized names, dates, key signatures, and such, but they do not provide a very good measure of students' understanding of how music works or their ability to make evaluative judgments about music. When we rely on simplistic ways to test learning, we are limited to teaching simplistic information about our art, and we may be denying our students opportunities for exciting, challenging, and meaningful learning experiences.

As part of the current education reform movement, teachers in all fields are discovering the advantages of authentic assessment tasks. In music, such tasks would require students to synthesize knowledge gained from instruction and use it to make informed decisions in their everyday listening. Ideally these situations will be relevant to the experiences in the students' daily lives and will help them assimilate the knowledge they've gained into their daily activities. In addition, well-written authentic assessment tasks let the students know

exactly what knowledge is being assessed and how their responses will be evaluated. This format eliminates students' having to second-guess the teacher and makes grading the work infinitely easier.

I have experimented with authentic assessment in my high school general music class and found the approach to be very successful for both me and my students. The two assessment items I am sharing with you were constructed to assess Music Standard 7A for grades 9–12: "Evaluating music and music performances: Students evolve specific criteria for making informed, critical evaluations of the quality and effectiveness of performances, compositions, arrangements, and improvisations and apply the criteria in their personal participation in music."

Assessing Music Criticism

My general music class includes a unit on music criticism. Early in the unit I make students aware of their role as music critics, as they select music for their daily listening and as they purchase tapes, CDs, and concert tickets. We also examine the concept of virtuosity, and students are asked to identify a living performer whom they believe will be considered a virtuoso. In the book *Music! Its Role and Importance in Our Lives* (Macmillan/McGraw-Hill, 1994), Charles Fowler defined virtuosos as "Persons who have extraordinary technical ability, beauty of sound, and personal charisma."

The first assessment tool I give students is a handout that describes the criteria that I will use to evaluate their work and also describes the project (see the Virtuoso Handout sidebar for the assessment portion of the handout). I then give

Virtuoso Handout Scoring Key

ARTIST: _____

Approach to work (4 pts.)   _____

Time (3 pts.)   _____

Format

    Bibliographic Information (2 pts.)   _____

    Music Information (3 pts.)   _____

    Justification (5 pts.)   _____

    Recorded/Video Example (3 pts.)   _____

                    Grade _____%

students two class periods to work in the library to conduct research for an oral report to be presented to the class. It is important to note that the students' presentation is to include a recorded demonstration of the musician's virtuosity. Also, make it clear that the scoring is weighted to emphasize the students' justification—that is the crux of the task.

I conclude the unit on music criticism by having students read and discuss several examples of professional criticism. To assess their learning within the unit, I have designed the second assessment tool—a task (described in the Unified Fine Arts sidebar) that I believe meets the criteria for authentic assessment; that is, it requires students to synthesize skills and knowledge gained in the unit, provides an opportunity for students to apply skills and knowledge to solve a realistic problem, and presents a task that is typical of tasks students perform in their everyday lives.

I provide a clear description of the task and give students sufficient direction to complete it. I also give them the scoring key when I make the assignment because it is important that they be aware of the criteria that will be used to evaluate their reviews. I devote an entire class period to this assessment task, beginning by giving students about two minutes to read the entire assignment. I then play the recording twice, encouraging them to listen the first time and take notes the second. Each student, however, has his or her own working style, and so I do not insist on any particular approach. After students have had ten to fifteen minutes to write, I play the recording again, and then for a fourth time eight to ten minutes before the end of the class period. This is emphasizing the importance of listening and reinforcing my belief that the review should be based on what students hear, not on what they know about the artist or the musical style.

Selecting the recording is critical, so I use the following criteria:

- The music should be in a popular genre that is familiar to most students.
- The music should be a new release that is

Unified Fine Arts Music Review

You are a critic for MTV. How would you review this new recording?

Here are some guidelines for writing your first music review:
1. Base your review on the merits of the recording as compared with the best of its kind.

2. Take a clear stance—either positive or negative. Make it clear to the reader where you stand and why.

3. Refer to the "critical words" you listed in the analysis of the Perlman and Wagner reviews. Use this list as a starting point for your writing. Add words to the list that describe this music.

4. The justification of your opinion must be music-specific. Avoid vague conmment, such as, "It's good." You must include two music-specific reasons for your opinions.

5. Format your review in three paragraphs:
   Paragraph 1 Identify the recording and artist(s); state your opinion.
   Paragraph 2 Justify your opinion, citing specific examples.
   Paragraph 3 Summarize.

Scoring Key		
Format	(3 pts.)	_____
Use of Critical Words	(2 pts.)	_____
Clear Stance	(5 pts.)	_____
Justification	(10 pts.)	_____
	Grade _____%	

CREATE YOUR REVIEW ON THE BACK OF THIS PAPER.

probably unfamiliar to most students (I recommend waiting until the day before the test to purchase the recording).

Authentic assessment tasks require a great deal of thought in their writing and in the building of the scoring instrument. Class activities can serve as the genesis for assessment items, which should be considered works in progress, because each time they are administered weaknesses appear that can be corrected.

Students respond well to these assessment tasks. They become engaged in the justification of their opinions because the context is meaningful to them. The thoughtful character of their responses is very rewarding. And nothing makes a teacher feel better than a student saying, "I wish all teachers gave tests like this!"

Victoria Smith is assistant professor of music education at Elizabethtown College in Elizabethtown, Pennsylvania. This article originally appeared in the Fall 1995 issue of General Music Today. *Reprinted by permission.*

Assessment in Instrumental Music Education—The Watkins-Farnum Performance Scale: An Old Friend Revisited

by Ronald E. Stitt

Asmus (1999) defines assessment as gathering, analyzing, interpreting and applying information about students that is then used to make decisions about educational programs involving those students. Colwell (1970) wrote that evaluation is constantly used in the process of living. Humans are always asking, "How am I doing?" and "How can I do better?" He defined evaluation as making a decision about the quality of that which is being evaluated.

Evaluation then could be considered to be a judgment of the worth of an experience, idea, process or product. An important part of the evaluation process is assessment. A common misconception is that a test, one type of assessment, can be used as the total basis for assessment. It must be clearly stated that this is untrue. Tests can provide information that can help the teacher in the assessment process but cannot be the sole source of assessment.

Radocy and Boyle (1987) suggest that assessment in music education will be more accurate if as much information as possible, both subjective and objective, is available to the teacher. In assessing musical performance, it must be remembered that the process is very subjective, as the musical sounds are processed by the listener's brain. While it is desirable to be as objective as possible when assessing musical performances, it will never be possible to eliminate the subjective aspects.

In any discussion of assessment of musical performance, two questions must be addressed:

(1) What should be assessed? and (2) How should it be assessed? In considering what should be assessed, it is necessary to decide whether to assess the overall performance or specific parts of the performance. The person(s) responsible for assessing the performance must decide the basis for the assessment and if "nonmusical elements" are to be included in the assessment process. Once these decisions are made, the "how" question can be answered.

According to Asmus (1999), an important element in the assessment process involves deciding what type of assessment to use. Authentic assessment is based upon information gathered from students who are performing tasks in real-life circumstances. This type of assessment works very well in instrumental music education. The teacher can choose from a number of assessment models including criterion-referenced, where the value of the student's performance is determined by comparing the performance to requirements that are established before the performance, or norms-referenced, where the value of the student's performance is determined by comparing to norms established previously and comparing the relationship of the student's performance to the norms.

In order for assessment to be reliable and valid, it must involve gathering data obtained from observation of student's performance, which can then be analyzed in order to make informed decisions about the teaching and learning that is occurring. Time-tested tools for collecting these data include, but are not limited to, the following:

Summative scales, also known as Likert scales, can be used to assess musical performance. Radocy and Boyle state that the Likert scale has an underlying continuum between two extremes. The judge (or teacher) listens to a performance and indicates his or her placement of the performance by circling a number or letter or by checking a location along a line. Most often, a specific aspect of the performance is identified by a statement that is intended to focus the response of the listener. The list of statements in Table 1 could be used in assessing musical performance with a Likert scale.

Table 1. Statement Scale for Assessing a Musical Performance

Tempo was steady	SA A N D SD
Phrasing was appropriate	SA A N D SD
Dynamic interpretation was accurate	SA A N D SD

The listener would circle letters ranging from strongly agree (SA) to strongly disagree (SD). A reliable Likert scale is an appropriate assessment tool when assessing specific parts of a performance.

Another type of scale that can be used is the semantic differential scale. A set of opposite-meaning adjectives should be constructed as shown below. The listener's ratings could be averaged for each performance to determine the ranking of the performer.

Table 2. Semantic Differential Scale for Assessing a Performer

mellow	___	___	___	___	___	harsh
in tune	___	___	___	___	___	out of tune
accurate	___	___	___	___	___	inaccurate
	1	2	3	4	5	

Another assessment is simply to rank in order of the listener's subjective, informal judgment. This tool can focus on overall performance, resulting in one or more scores being given for a number of specific areas and then added together to obtain a total score. If more than one listener is involved in the process, scores can be averaged or added together.

The techniques for assessing performance discussed above are all frequently used and give the listener (teacher) the freedom to work specific criteria into the system. What one person considers important or representative of a musical perform-

ance will not always match another person's view. With these types of assessment tools, this is inevitable, and, when completing the assessment of a performance, this must be kept in mind. Also, performances cannot be compared when evaluations come from a variety of sources using these types of non-standardized assessment tools.

The Watkins-Farnum Performance Scale (WFPS, 1962) may be a solution to obtaining objective assessment of music performance. This achievement test is a standardized test of music performance first published in 1954 and then revised in 1962. It is designed to assess performance and progress of performers on wind instruments and snare drum using prepared music and in sight-reading skills. Performers are required to play printed music that becomes progressively more difficult. The performer continues to play as far into the exercises as possible until excessive errors are made. Although the WFPS is nearly forty years old, it may still be used with confidence to fill the need for assessing instrumental performance.

Directions in the WFPS manual clearly explain the rules for scoring the scale, the types of errors that should be considered and the instructions to the student. The scale must be administered individually. A brief, but informative discussion reports the reliability and validity of the scale. These data indicate that the scale can be used with confidence. The scale's book, in both Form A and Form B (two different versions of the scale), includes the exercises for each instrument. Also available are scoring sheets for each instrument to track and record data about each performance. The exercises are included on this scoring sheet also. The two forms of the scale correlate at .982. This scale seems to be as objective as possible in the nature of errors to be considered in the scoring. Subjective aspects of a performance, such as tone quality, are not addressed in the scoring. In spite of criticisms that may be and have been made of this scale, it does have value in that it provides a norms-sampled, standardized scale for assessing players from different programs.

As mentioned at the beginning of this discussion, testing is just one part of the evaluation. Music educators are called upon to make evaluations for many reasons. Performing ensemble directors can and should use a variety of assessment tools to help make their assessment of students as accurate as possible.

A variety of uses exists for these tools. Student selection to a performing ensemble can be one application. Once personnel are selected, seating placement within the ensemble can be determined with the help of these tools. Assessing sight-reading ability is another application that can be useful. Assessing individual progress for the purpose of grading and/or advancement in a performance curriculum is yet another way that these tools can be applied. Teachers can use the information obtained from these assessment tools to help in designing and individualizing instruction for their students. Tracking progress and noting where difficulties occur can be a valuable aid in organizing appropriate instruction to meet the needs of the individual students as well as the ensemble as a whole.

When to administer these assessment tools can vary depending on what information is being sought and the purpose to be served by this information. I would suggest that a full battery of assessment tools be given at the beginning of the year to establish benchmarks. The tests should then be given at the end of the year in order to obtain data showing progress that has been made. During the school year, shorter versions of the assessment tools can be employed in order to ensure that each student's progress is being tracked and accounted for. If grades are to be based on these interim assessments, enough of, and the correct types of, criteria must be included in order to make accurate assessment possible.

According to Goolsby (1999), "Our task is to produce better musicians, and better musicians will produce better music." When reliable and valid assessment tools are correctly administered, assessment can be a valuable teaching tool and the teaching-learning situation should be improved. When teaching is effective and appropriate, learning has the best chance to be successful. And when students learn successfully, they will feel good about themselves and what they have accomplished. What more can a teacher ask?

References

Asmus, E. P. (1999). Music assessment concepts. *Music Educators Journal, 86* (2), 19–24.

Boyle, J. D., & Radocy, R. E. (1987). *Measurement and evaluation of musical experience.* New York: Schirmer Books.

Colwell, R. J. (1970). *The Evaluation of music teaching and learning.* Englewood Cliffs, NJ: Prentice Hall.

Goolsby, T. W. (1999). Assessment in instrumental music. *Music Educators Journal, 86* (2), 31–35, 50.

Watkins, J. G., & Farnum, S. E. (1962). *The Watkins-Farnum performance scale: Form B.* Winona, MN: Hal Leonard.

Ronald E. Stitt teaches instrumental music at Fort LeBoeuf Middle School in Waterford, Pennsylvania. This article originally appeared in the Winter 1999–2000 issue of PMEA News. Reprinted by permission.

Assessment: An Integral Part of Instruction

by Garry J. Walker

For the majority of my teaching career, when I heard the word "assessment," I immediately thought "test." When I thought about tests, I thought about a meaningful way to arrive at a grade in my class.

It is important to remember that the Latin root of assess (assidere) means "to sit beside." Assessment is the process of collecting, describing and analyzing information about performance. Although some assessments may result from a series of tests, most people do not produce their best work under test-like conditions.

Performance-based assessment requires students to perform a task rather than simply answer questions. The central defining element in all performance assessment methods is that the test taker creates an *answer product* to demonstrate knowledge or skills in a particular field. It is not a single-letter grade applied at the end of each marking period. The assessed activity is itself a real-world performance, with relevance to the student and to the community. In a fair performance-based system, the student has repeated opportunities to meet or exceed the standards.

The definitions contained in the previous two paragraphs are taken from *SCASS Arts Assessment Project Glossary of Assessment Terms.*[1] The settings found in music performance classes provide a rich environment for the use of ongoing assessment of student progress toward standards both in skill development and understanding musical concepts. In order to make the learning richer and longer lasting for the students, the criteria for success need to be clear and attainable.

For example, the traditional playing/singing test provides an opportunity for students to demonstrate what they know in terms of the music being prepared for performance. The key to the value and effectiveness of this kind of assessment is clear criteria and standards. Specifically, what will be assessed in the exercise? Will it include an evaluation of accuracy only on notes and rhythms, or will it also deal with tone quality, phrasing, intonation, articulation and style? If all of the musical elements listed are being assessed, what defines the standard for different levels of attainment for each of these elements? When students have a clear understanding of the criteria, they will reach higher standards than if they are only told to be prepared for a performance test on the section from A to B on a selected piece.

In order to be most effective in instruction, it is important to determine the level of prior learning for each student. For example, if a group has trouble sight-reading, it is important to determine why on an individual basis. Some groups who sight read poorly may perform quite well given enough time to drill and practice. The problem with the drill and practice approach is that it doesn't develop good sight-reading skill. By creating some fairly simple assessments to determine where the lack of understanding exists and developing strategies to enable the students to learn the necessary skills, the students can become successful sight-readers in a fairly short amount of time.

In the case of sight-reading, the assessment process might look like:

- Take rhythms from the sight-reading music to create a practice sheet to be performed on a single pitch. Play these rhythms as a group to determine if the problem is the ability to count the rhythm or other challenges in the music.
- If the students are unsuccessful in reading the rhythms, develop another sheet with similar rhythms. Have each student write in the beats

including subdivision. This will provide clear information about individual understanding of rhythm.

- Using information from the counting exercise, develop some practice tools to be used in warm-up and other activities to help students learn the skills they are lacking.

The important element in this short scenario is the individual assessment of the ability to count. The results of the exercise provide specific information about individual strengths and weaknesses. A quote from Michael Riley, superintendent of schools in Bellevue, Washington, sums up the need for this kind of assessment quite clearly:

> What we learn from our analysis of student work should inform our actions. It may result in additional help for students who need it, or extensions for students who are ready for them. It may lead to our changing or refining materials and teaching techniques. It may cause us to change the sequencing of lessons so the students are provided with the prerequisite skill they need. **No lesson is perfect. Therefore, no curriculum is ever complete**.[2]

Before you design any assessment tool, you need to clearly define the learning target to be assessed. For example, if you were going to develop a rubric to assess tone quality, the learning target would be producing a quality tone appropriate for age, development and medium. The rubric would contain the key characteristics for tone and a clear description of what tone would sound like at each level of the rubric.

Alignment is essential. The tools you design to assess any learning must reflect instruction. If the activity used to assess or the material being assessed does not match what the students have learned in class, the assessment is invalid.

One of the most important considerations is choosing the appropriate and most efficient tool for assessing the specific learning. Matching or fill-in-the-blank tests would be most efficient for assessing knowledge of music terminology. A check sheet can document that a task was completed, and rating scales can measure progress toward a goal, with descriptions as well as numbers ranging from 1 to 10.

It is important to understand the difference between assessments you use in making instructional decisions on a daily basis and the tools used for district, state or national assessments. The assessment of regular student progress is used to make instructional decisions to enhance the learning for each student. Large-scale assessments are used to make decisions about programs and school districts based on statewide standards. Large-scale assessments take snapshots that only reflect a small portion of the total learning that takes place in each program.

If assessment based on clear criteria to measure both skill development and the ability to transfer concepts exists in each music classroom in the state, our students will be well prepared for any large-scale assessment that may become a part of the educational process in the future.

Notes
1. Council of Chief State School Officers, "Glossary of Assessment Terms," Proceedings of State Collaborative on Assessment and Student Standards/Arts Education Assessment Consortium, Hidden Valley, PA, July 28–August 2, 1998.

2. Dr. Michael Riley [Superintendent of Schools, Bellevue Public Schools], School District Workshop Handout. Bellevue, WA, 1998.

Garry Walker teaches orchestra at Newport High School in Bellevue, Washington, is adjunct professor of secondary music education at Seattle Pacific University in Seattle, and served as a state representative at the SCASS Institute on Assessment in the Arts. This article originally appeared in the March 1999 issue of Washington's Voice. *Reprinted by permission.*

Curriculum, Instruction and Assessment: There Is a Link

by Richard Wells

As school systems across the United States revise their curriculum in light of the National Standards, there has been an increased focus on the role of assessment in music education. National, state and local districts have become interested in determining to what extent students are meeting these standards. However, as we become more assessment-conscious, we must not forget to place the role of assessment in a larger context. Curriculum, instruction and assessment are all equal partners in the educational process, and they are all interrelated and equally important. Viewing assessment by itself may be shortsighted and may not lead students to learn.

Curriculum

Curriculum development is a critical component in the assessment process. Unless we clearly determine what we want students to know and be able to do, how can we carry out an assessment? The National Standards can certainly guide the curriculum development process. However, for curriculum as well as instruction and assessment, the Standards need to be further defined. We need to have specific answers to these two questions:

• What types of activities or tasks should our students engage in in our music classes?
• What should we look at or listen to in order to determine if they have been successful?

The standards do not provide complete answers to these questions. Therefore, individual school systems need to devote time to operationalizing these standards through curriculum development that reflects local needs, resources and expertise.

The types of activities or tasks we ask students to participate in at the district level may be quite different from school to school. These will be affected by the different methodologies that teachers use. Orff teachers, for example, may choose somewhat different activities than Kodály teachers. The background of students also will influence the types of activities that are used in classes. Teachers who have students of a particular ethnic background may use this as a resource in their teaching. Finally, probably the most significant difference controlling the types of activities that are used in classes is the amount of resources each school system provides. This will include the amount of time that students have music each week as well as other resources such as equipment and facilities. The items above represent some of the factors that will need to be taken into account by each school district as it develops its curriculum. The result of this work will have a major impact on classroom instruction, as well as assessment.

Besides giving parameters for activities and tasks, curriculum should also identify the assessment dimensions, or what we should look at or listen to, when determining if a student has been successful in a particular task or activity. Identifying these dimensions will obviously be very helpful in the assessment process. However, often curriculum documents overlook this component. They merely become a list of activities:

- Students will sing canons, rounds and partner songs.
- Students will listen to music from a variety of cultures.
- Students will compose sound effects for poems.

The effectiveness of our instruction and assessment will certainly be impacted if we do not clearly know what we need to look at or listen to when determining if students are successful.

Instruction

Most of the planning we do as teachers consists of developing instructional units or lesson plans. Although the extent of day-to-day written lesson plans may vary from teacher to teacher, there should be a conscious effort on behalf of all teachers to develop thoughtful lessons that are linked to a curriculum. Teachers should ask questions, such as:

- What are the best approaches or methods for teaching specific knowledge or skills?
- Is my instruction linked to the curriculum?

Without thoughtful lesson planning, we can easily fall into the practice of developing lesson plans without asking either of the above questions. We may find ourselves using exciting lesson ideas gleaned from a publication or workshop that fail to move students toward meeting our curricular objectives. If we do not consult our curriculum, we may at the end of the year find we have exposed students to a number of fun activities that fall short of covering the breadth and depth of our curriculum. As a result, assessment will become a very difficult or frustrating process.

Assessment

Both curriculum and instruction have an influence on the nature of our assessments. When curriculum and instruction are well thought out, assessment is not a difficult process. Assessment should:

- be a regular part of instruction.
- be based on authentic tasks that represent what "real musicians" do. The parameters for these tasks should be outlined in the curriculum and carried out in our instruction.
- give students a role in the assessment process.

We find that the best assessments are those that are imbedded in the instruction. Assessment should occur in every class as the teacher monitors and adjusts instruction. When students are formally assessed they should not be given tasks that are foreign to them. For example, it would obviously be unfair to administer a sight-reading test to students if you have not devoted time to sight-reading in your class.

I remember the days when attendance and behavior were the major component of grades. This may have been the case because it was the easiest to measure, especially when curriculum was not well-defined. We should not limit ourselves, however, to behavior or to pencil-and-paper tests just because they might be easy to grade. We should identify the most important skills that students need to learn and then develop ways to assess them. We may need to consider using portfolios, including video- or audiocassette formats, written performance critiques by students, and self- and peer-assessments.

We also need to ask ourselves, "Is this the type of task that real musicians engage in?" Although there is a place for "building-block assessments" such as doing scales, rhythmic or tonal patterns, these should lead to assessments using "real" music or melodies. If we do not use authentic tasks, we may be teaching students skills that they will never use in the "real world."

It is important for us to give students a major role in the assessment process. Student self-assessment should be a major objective for music education. In fact, one might even argue that the role of education is to teach students to be self-reflective. When students self-assess, they can take charge of their own learning. They can set goals with the help of the teachers and work toward these on their own. The benefit is that, when students become independent learners, their potential growth increases dramatically. The time taken from class doing this type of assessment is more than made up for over the course of a semester.

Teachers who use self-assessment find that it changes their instruction. They frequently ask students to identify the strengths and weaknesses in their performances or compositions. "What's wrong during that section, trumpets?" They also ask students to identify strategies for improvement. "How are you going to fix the intonation in that section?" Compare this to "Trumpets, how many times have I told you to play softer during that section?" or "Trumpets, how many times have

I told you your low 'D' is always sharp? When are you going to get your third-finger tuning slide fixed?" In the latter example, the teacher is not giving the students responsibility for their own learning.

As can be seen, the educational process is strengthened when curriculum, instruction and assessment are interrelated. Each plays an important role. Assessment is most effective when curriculum and instruction are well developed.

Richard Wells teaches in the Simsbury Public Schools in Simsbury, Connecticut. This article, which appears here in slightly abridged form, originally appeared in the Spring 1998 issue of Connecticut's CMEA News. *Reprinted by permission.*

Multitrack Cassette Recorders: A Technology for Assessment

by Charles Rochester Young and David Regenberg

A musician's performance cannot exceed the musical performance in his or her own mind, whether conscious, subconscious, or superconscious. Therefore, the mind and ear need continuous training for performance development to occur. Curiously, many schools' computer music labs are not designed for performance development, even though performing ensembles comprise the majority of their curricula. (Just imagine the problems a student composer would have hearing while sitting in a lab next to a timpanist!) Multitrack cassette recorders solve this dilemma because they are portable and effective in a computer music lab *or* in a classroom, concert hall, and/or practice room. Unlike keyboard labs, multitrack cassette recorders also allow students to use tools, such as their instruments and voices, with which they are already familiar. For these reasons, the multitrack cassette recorder proves itself to be a tremendously flexible and powerful tool for musicians to develop fundamentals.

A multitrack cassette recorder is a multitrack cassette deck and a mixer joined into one device. **This device makes maximum use of the greatest music-making tool in the universe—THE HUMAN EAR!** Curricula utilizing multitrack recording uniquely and effectively assist in the development of listening, expression and technical performance skills. In these curricula, students have the opportunity to immediately listen to their recorded exercises and performance(s) for the purpose of self-assessment. However, what musicians "hear" and what they "think they hear" are often different things, since they are both critic and creator. Multitrack recordings solve this problem, serving as a mirror with a virtually infinite time frame. Therefore, a student should spend time listening to his or her original performance, allowing for more objective assessment over time. Experience has taught us that thorough recording analysis develops skills faster than otherwise. Over time, multitrack recording will continually narrow the gap between a musician's perception and reality and develop the musician's performance to a level more consistent with his or her mental and aural concepts. It is indeed a rare individual who can narrow that gap with only his or her internal devices. Multitrack cassette recorders allow students to work at their most effective pace and become more responsible for their own learning.

Unlike other cassette recorders, **multitrack cassette recorders allow students to record ALL of the parts in a piece by themselves and listen to each individual part in isolation or in combination.** By having students perform and assess ALL of the parts in a piece, such as a Bach chorale, they become more musical and more aware of subtle details and relationships. Since students are reading directly from a score, they learn to think and hear beyond their own parts. Issues such as intonation, balance, blend, rhythmic alignment, and phrasing between the parts become more important as a result.

Throughout each assignment, students and faculty work independently and in various combinations to create a positive and nurturing atmosphere. Students are required to detect errors in their performances and develop "rehearsal" plans for improvement. These issues are accomplished using a self-assessment worksheet that dissects the performance into components such as tempo, rhythm, dynamics, articulation, vibrato, intonation, and timbre. The self-assessments also allow the teacher an opportunity to assess student development throughout the assignment, rather than relying exclusively on a final tape. This "process-based" orientation leads to better understanding and a better "product."

Once satisfied with their performance, students submit their final tapes and self-assessments to the instructor. Grades are earned for the taped performance *and* the accuracy of their self-assessment. These media ultimately reflect EVERYTHING the student understands about music-making. As a result, teachers assess the students' comprehensive musicianship better than through traditional written assignments where the responsibility for assessment lies exclusively with the teacher. These final tapes and self-assessments can also be archived for the students, faculty, administration, and parents to observe progress outside of class.

Students have commented that self-assessments improved their play in an ensemble, taught them to listen to themselves, and helped them deal with frustration better. Others commented that the assignments allowed them to see exactly where they stood as a comprehensive musician. A sophomore music education (flute) student said, "I loved this assignment and found the process quite helpful. The transcription of the artist on the recording was particularly helpful for analyzing expression. I also learned a lot about ensemble playing, part-writing, rhythm, and my overall sound. Unfortunately, I also found out that I don't always sing in tune with my own playing, although I did get

better. All of this information will be extremely useful in the future." Some students have also enjoyed the creative opportunities afforded through the assignments. Students have been known to identify their tapes through four-part vocal harmony or through original compositions using their names as motives. Other students have commented on the satisfaction they feel by producing recordings themselves. These moments of achievement are memorable and exhilarating!

To commence multitrack cassette recording, you need a tape, microphone, microphone stand, multitrack cassette recorder, and headphones. **All of this equipment can be purchased from a variety of companies in a package for under $600.** Any device with a one-fourth inch audio output (drum machines or metronomes, tuners, and synthesizers) can also be implemented along with the multitrack cassette recorder to reinforce quality practice habits and promote student inquiry. The technology is relatively easy to use, and students can be trained in an hour. With consistent use, students can ultimately concentrate on the musical issues at hand rather than the technology.

If there are any questions about multitrack recording, assignments that employ this techology or self-assessment worksheets, feel free to contact me at UW–Stevens Point.

Charles Rochester Young is chair of composition and music theory and director of the Computer Music Center at the University of Wisconsin at Stevens Point. David Regenberg is president of U.S. Masters Guitar Works in Middleton, Wisconsin. This article originally appeared in the September 1998 issue of Wisconsin School Musician. *Reprinted by permission.*

Other MENC Resources for Assessment in Music Education

An Agenda for Excellence in Music at the Middle Level. 1994. 24 pages. #1629

Aiming for Excellence: The Impact of the Standards Movement on Music Education. 1996. 160 pages. #1012.

Assessing Student Learning: A Practical Guide (CD-Rom) edited by Kent Seidel. A publication of the Alliance for Curriculum Reform. 2000. #3008.

Assessing Student Learning: New Rules, New Realities edited by Ronald S. Brandt. A publication of the Alliance for Curriculum Reform. 1998. 110 pages #1661.

Guide to Evaluating Teachers of Music Performance Groups by David P. Doerkson. 1990. 72 pages. #1017.

Guidelines for Performances of School Music Groups: Expectations and Limitations prepared by the MENC Committee on Standards. 1986. 44 pages. #1016.

National Standards for Arts Education: What Every Young American Should Know and Be Able to Do in the Arts developed by the Consortium of National Arts Education Associations. 1994. 148 pages. #1605.

Opportunity-to-Learn Standards for Arts Education. 1995. 64 pages. #1643.

Opportunity-to-Learn Standards for Music Instruction: Grades PreK–12 developed by MENC, project director Paul R. Lehman. 1994. 32 pages. #1619.

Performance Standards for Music: Strategies and Benchmarks for Assessing Progress toward the National Standards, Grades PreK–12 developed by the MENC Committee on Performance Standards, chaired by Paul R. Lehman. 1996. 136 pages. #1633.

Performing with Understanding: The Challenge of the National Standards for Music Education edited by Bennet Reimer. 2000. 216 pages. #1672.

Perspectives on Implementation: Arts Education Standards for America's Students. 1994. 128 pages. #1622.

Prekindergarten Music Education Standards (brochure). 1995. #4015.

The School Music Program—A New Vision: The K–12 National Standards, PreK Standards, and What They Mean to Music Educators developed by the MENC Task Force for National Standards in the Arts, chaired by Paul R. Lehman. 1994. 48 pages. #1618.

For complete ordering information on these and other publications, contact:

MENC Publications Sales
1806 Robert Fulton Drive
Reston, VA 20191-4348

Credit card holders may call 1-800-828-0229.

Spotlight

on
Assessment in
Music Education

Made in the USA
Lexington, KY
19 August 2016